THE PERFECT BOOK FOR

DAD

THE PERFECT BOOK FOR

DAD

The Astonishingly Complete Guide to Fatherhood

Paul Barker

HARPER

ENTERTAINMENT

An Imprint of HarperCollinsPublishers

FIRST U.S. EDITION

Illustrations by Matt Blease

Library of Congress Cataloging-in-Publication Data has been applied for.

ISBN 978-0-06-145072-3

08 09 10 11 12 WBC/RRD 10 9 8 7 6 5 4 3 2 1

For Bill

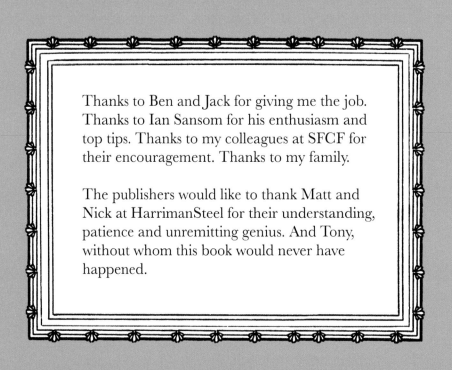

Thanks to Ben and Jack for giving me the job.
Thanks to Ian Sansom for his enthusiasm and
top tips. Thanks to my colleagues at SFCF for
their encouragement. Thanks to my family.

The publishers would like to thank Matt and
Nick at HarrimanSteel for their understanding,
patience and unremitting genius. And Tony,
without whom this book would never have
happened.

Contents

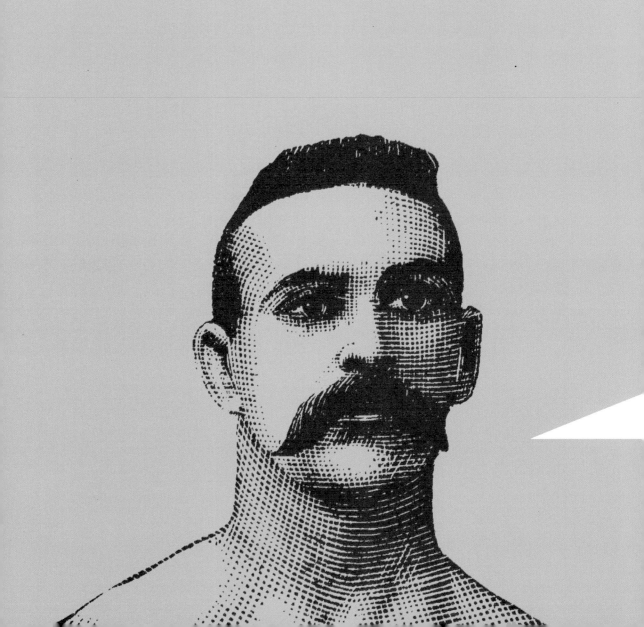

Foreword: Who Is Dad?

Dad. Say it. Dad. What does "dad" mean? Dad's not father. No. Not papa. Definitely not. Not daddy, not daddio. No way. Don't even consider pater. Dad is something and someone else entirely. Dad. He has a solid monosyllabic quality, a comforting bluntness. Dad is all homely and informal in his open-necked shirt. Dad is unique and universal, a fascinating amalgam of qualities, vices and foibles. Dad is drama and excitement, unfolding action, comedy, romance, soap opera, game show. All human life is in "dad." Dad is a landscape and a portrait. Dad is history; dad is culture. Dad reaches his arms around the world. Dad is a king with an invisible crown. Dad is the center of gravity, the slowly spinning gyroscope from which all things come. Dad is all this and more. Pretty much.

You might be a dad; you might not. But, whoever you are, rich or poor, black or white, great or small, man, woman or child, you will know how essential dad can be. You will know of an occasion, an incident, an accident, something from your very own past that says something about the nature, the role, the purpose of dad. Dad is part of nature's great cycle. Dads have children; children have dads. And so on. It's time to celebrate dad.

PART
ONE

Know Your Dad

Know Your Dad

Dads are, of course, people. For this reason, dads and expressions of dadness are infinitely varied. But, infinitely varied or not, they can be analyzed and assessed, and many fall into recognizable patterns of behavior. So, if you're trying to figure out exactly who and what your dad is, or you are a dad and you're trying to figure out exactly who and what you are, or you are a dad and you know exactly who and what you are but you're thinking of reinventing yourself, then it's worth making brain-space for the types of dad available.

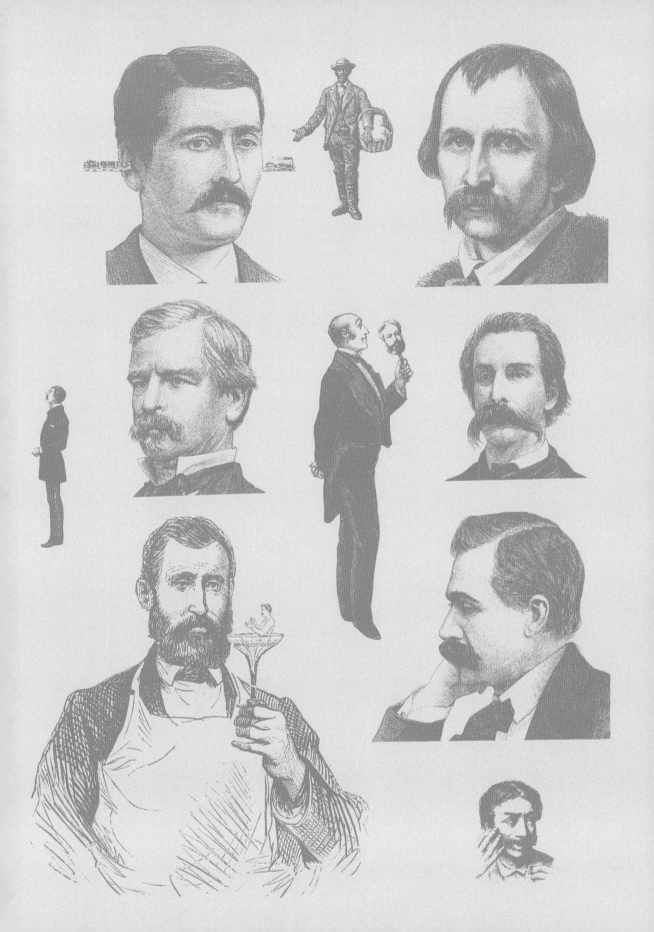

How Strict Is Your Dad?

Your dad finds the twelve-year-old you smoking a Camel in the shed. His response is to . . .

a) Enlist you in the navy.

b) Withdraw library privileges for a month.

c) Say, without looking at you, "Camels are for the servants. You should have asked me."

If you answered:

a) Your dad is pretty strict. At least he lets you live.

b) Your dad is pretty savvy—he knew you'd prefer a caning to get it over with.

c) Your dad may not be your real father.

Dad Rule

Dads come in different levels of scariness— some can be tyrants, others are more like big cuddly toys you take money from. Some can fail to instill any morals at all.

How Fashionable Is Your Dad?

Your parents are invited to a friend's fortieth-birthday bash. Your dad wears . . .

a) That somewhat somber suit he wore when he appeared before the Senate Select Committee.

b) His Rolling Stones Voodoo Lounge Tour T-shirt.

c) The ironed top and trousers your mom put out for him.

If you answered:

a) Your dad is not very fashionable, but it's okay because he really doesn't care.

b) The answer is the same.

c) Your dad could possibly be quite . . . "cool." In this case it all depends on your mother.

Dad Rule

There is a very general and very simple rule when it comes to dads and fashion—they are not fashionable.

How Old Is Your Dad?

You run to your dad, new soccer ball in hand, and beg him to come outside for a game. Your dad . . .

a) Has snatched the ball from you and has dribbled halfway down the driveway before you have laced up your shoes.

b) Lowers the *New York Times*, puts down his pipe and says, "That's more of a weekend sort of thing, bud. I've been working, so I just want to read the obits, puff the old St. Bruno and sip on a single malt. All right?"

c) Does nothing. But the nurse beside the bed puts her finger to her lips and shakes her head.

If you answered:

a) Your dad is still plenty youthful and good for all the outdoor stuff.

b) Your dad is probably past his peak, but good for the occasional outing. If you have two older siblings you are very likely an accident.

c) It sounds like you could be accidental or illegitimate. Either way, you're playing alone.

Dad Rule

Dads are not constrained by biology in the same ways that moms are. There have been some famous octogenarian dads with plenty to offer (mostly cash).

How Left Wing Is Your Dad?

A man canvassing for an extreme right-wing party comes to the door. Your dad . . .

a) Punches him on the nose.

b) Tries to punch him on the nose but fails.

c) Says he doesn't believe in God, thank you very much, and closes the door.

If you answered:

a) Your dad is probably more violent than ideologically committed.

b) Your dad is probably committed but inept.

c) There are a number of possibilities, including the possibility that your dad is highly committed but frequently drunk.

Dad Rule

Left-wing dads are becoming increasingly rare. These days you are more likely to have a generally anti-capitalist dad. If you have got the genuine article, treasure him—he's highly collectible.

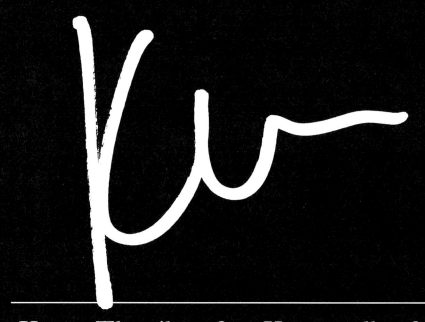

Ken—The silver fox, Ken smells of new and
cheap leather sofas. An impressive covering of
chest hair belies a sharp intellect and a lateral-
thinking mind; perfect for the Sunday *Times*
crossword. Myopic to the point of absurdity, Ken's
glasses would happily withstand a lunar reentry.

How Puerile Is Your Dad?

The presenters of a wildlife TV program are discussing "a beautiful pair of tits." Your dad . . .

a) Snorts his soup out through his nose.

b) Says, "The one on the left looks a good deal more plump."

c) Says, "Yes."

If you answered:

a) Your dad is puerile, but only averagely so.

b) Your dad is clearly highly suggestible and could be dangerous.

c) You are the proud possessor of an ambiguous dad. Ambiguous dads can be great fun.

Dad Rule

Generally speaking, a puerile dad tends to be a bit annoying. Most dads understand that puerility is immature and that's not what your kids want from you.

How Punctual Is Your Dad?

Your dad has an important meeting at 9 a.m. He . . .

a) Leaves an hour early in case the first train is canceled or delayed.

b) Contributes to the meeting by cell phone from the parking lot of a Taco Bell.

c) Has his presentation available as a download from a dedicated Internet site, and is available for questions via live webcam conferencing.

If you answered:

a) Your dad is a sound, punctual man who takes his responsibilities seriously.

b) Your dad may have good intentions, but he has no strategy.

c) Your dad doesn't need to be punctual because he's living in the future.

Dad Rule

A punctual dad is a good dad—especially after football practice, the movies, the school dance or a five-hour bender in a nightclub.

What Does Your Dad Always Carry with Him?

On the way back from a weekend in Vermont, the family car breaks down at night on the highway. Your dad produces his . . .

a) Tool kit. He then busies himself under the hood for a couple of minutes before returning to the car, starting it the first time and muttering, "Thought so," to himself.

b) SAS survival manual. He then gets everybody out of the car and begins the search for "high ground and cover."

c) Guitar. He then gives the family a heartfelt rendition of "Stairway to Heaven."

If you answered:

a) Your dad is awesome and, even though he might spend much of his time in the garage, is definitely a handy dad in a crisis.

b) Your dad is probably fairly good in a sticky situation, but may overreact. A dogged, level-headed mom helps in such cases.

c) Your dad is really entertaining to have around, but may not be able to keep you alive in a mortal danger scenario.

Dad Rule

Most dads carry something with them, whether a pen or a copy of *Lyrical Ballads*. It helps them feel ready for something.

How Philosophical Is Your Dad?

The family is on a day trip to Boston when a weirdo approaches in the street and tells your dad that he is nothing more than a product of dominant ideology. Your dad replies . . .

a) "What do you mean by product? What do you mean by dominant? And what do you mean by ideology?"

b) "I'm already a member, thank you very much."

c) "Er . . ."

If you answered:

a) Your dad is probably a fairly philosophical fellow. At least he likes to settle the terms of reference.

b) Either your dad doesn't like being stopped in the street, or he's agreeing with the terms of reference in an ironic sort of way.

c) Your dad is probably not used to the cut and thrust of intellectual debate. He could still be a great guy, though.

Dad Rule

A philosophical dad is a good thing. Certainly he is more likely to understand any difficulties his children might have, rather than lashing out or shouting. Another good way of testing how philosophical your dad might be is to keep asking "why?" and see how long it takes him to lose his temper.

What Does Your Dad Call You?

Part One

Your dad comes home from a lengthy business trip. You are playing in the street and see him turn the corner, his briefcase in his hand. You run toward him, and beaming his most adoring smile, he opens his arms wide to receive you. He calls out . . .

a) "Hey, scout! Good to see you!"

b) "Hey, little monkey!"

c) "Hey, it's you!"

If you answered:

a) Your dad is Gregory Peck in *To Kill a Mockingbird*. That's rare. It's also excellent, as Gregory Peck plays a highly heroic dad in a film of a book in which a highly heroic dad is a central character.

b) Your dad sees you as something of a pet. At some point he will need disabusing of this idea.

c) Your dad probably can't remember your name. If you are one of numerous siblings, this is what you are probably used to. If you are an only child and your dad is often away on lengthy business trips, it's just possible that he's a bigamist, or at least living a double life.

Part Two

You have received an unusually poor report card and your dad summons you to the study to reprimand you. He calls out . . .

a) **Your full name. For example, John Prestatyn Erasmus Smith, or Emily Rosamund Mooncalf Jones.**

b) **(Depending on gender) simply "Boy" or "Girl."**

c) **"Yo, loser!"**

If you answered:

a) Your dad is okay. He just wants you to see yourself as a full person, as someone who should have some self-respect, someone who should want to fulfill his or her intellectual potential.

b) Your dad wants what dad (a) wants, he just can't remember your name.

c) Your dad takes a somewhat harsh attitude toward your accomplishments. Success *can* be achieved through fear of violent retribution, but it is a bit of an outdated approach.

Dad Rule

Sometimes what your dad calls you can say more about him than you. Don't be afraid to tell him if you find your given moniker inappropriate. Sometimes he just might not see that "Bell-end" is not a nickname all children will feel comfortable with.

How Financially Sound Is Your Dad?

Your dad comes into your room to "talk about money." He says . . .

a) "You're twelve years old now, we need to discuss the corporation and your inheritance."

b) "You're twelve years old now, which is old enough to lend your old man some cash. I need some smokes and I got a tip on the ponies."

c) "You're twelve years old now, so I'm giving you money to put aside for your wedding."

If you answered:

a) Your dad is probably rich. This is a good thing, in that having nothing is certainly worse, but, as poor people hope, it won't guarantee your dad happiness.

b) Your dad is financially challenged. Unfortunately, this type of dad often requires money as well as love, and rich and successful children are his favorite kind.

c) Your family may be the cast of a Dickens novel. So your dad is basically a good man who has fallen victim to a cruel, unsentimental world.

Dad Rule

Let's face it, in any child's view, dads are there to buy you things. So, the richer your dad, the better the things you get. It doesn't always work out, but the odds are not bad.

How Realistic Is Your Dad?

You are a young child, and as the festive season approaches, you question your dad about the existence of another father — Santa Claus. He says . . .

a) "Of course Santa Claus exists. And if you've been a good child, I'm sure he'll bring you all the presents you want."

b) "Santa Claus is a myth. If you're going to ask me about God—ditto. Any more questions?"

c) "Move out of the way. I'm watching the game."

If you answered:

a) Your dad likes dreams and fantasy. These kinds of dads tend not to be realistic but are usually pretty indulgent.

b) Your dad is one hard-nosed guy. He can seem harsh and uncaring at times and his children tend toward extremes—captains of industry or drug addicts.

c) Your dad also likes dreams and fantasy. Unfortunately, these dreams are of a financial nature. Your dad may be indulgent too, but not indefinitely.

Dad Rule

As with many dad qualities, compromise is best. You want a dad who is going to understand your dreams, even if they are genuinely stupid.

How Patriotic Is Your Dad?

Your dad is at a Yankees game with some work colleagues. When the players are lined up and the band strikes up the national anthem, your dad . . .

a) Stands up and is suddenly surprised by a tear in his eye.

b) Turns to the business section of the *Wall Street Journal.*

c) Slides his gaze along the line of players and shakes his head ruefully.

If you answered:

a) Your dad is the common passive patriot. He gets emotional, but not often.

b) Your dad is more committed to a bullish futures market than any particular country. This type of dad is often rich, which is good, but don't expect him ever to let you win at anything.

c) Your dad is looking to emigrate.

Dad Rule

Patriotism is the last refuge of the scoundrel. Dads can be scoundrels, so don't be surprised if the old man has an inner flag-waver.

How Indulgent Is Your Dad?

It's your eleventh birthday. As he hands you your present, he says . . .

a) "I know how much you like whiskey. I thought you should have some single malts of your own. You know, for when the guys are over and stuff."

b) "Now we're quits."

c) "Obviously, the personal butler is only a token. The real gift is in the card—I've listed the additions I've made to your stock portfolio."

If you answered:

a) Your dad is pretty indulgent. Single malts! What will your eighteenth be like?

b) You need to do some thinking. What did he mean? He certainly doesn't sound indulgent.

c) Your dad may seem way too indulgent but it would seem you're already living a rarefied life, in which case you're probably already used to it.

Dad Rule

An indulgent dad may sound like a good thing. He is.

Where Did It All Begin?

Your earliest memory of your dad is . . .

a) Him lying on a beach, a *National Enquirer* across his face and a strange noise coming from beneath it.

b) Him on TV, playing football.

c) Him coming home after being away for several months, and your mother crying and saying, "You're alive!" over and over again.

If you answered:

a) Your dad is just some guy. Makes you wonder why it is that *you* read the *Times*.

b) Anything is possible—he may be running a bar in Atlanta by now, he may be the trainer of a string of Preakness winners.

c) It sounds like you are always going to be living up to something major.

Dad Rule

Your earliest memory of your dad probably doesn't signify much. If it's good, then thinking about it from time to time might help reinforce familial bonds. If it's bad, then let it go. It was probably just dad on an off day.

So you think you know me?

PART
TWO

The
Spotter's
Guide

The Spotter's Guide

Walk down any street, avenue, lane, boulevard or alley, and you might well pass one. Buy an item in a store or call a hotline to complain about something, and you might well speak to one. Spill a pint in a bar and you might end up fighting one. Better still, get your binoculars and a pad and pencil and start spotting them. Dads. Like those finches that hang around the Galápagos Islands, dads adapt to all sorts of environmental factors. Spotting and identifying these adaptations can almost make for a fascinating hobby or pastime. You might find that you know one. You might even find that you are one.

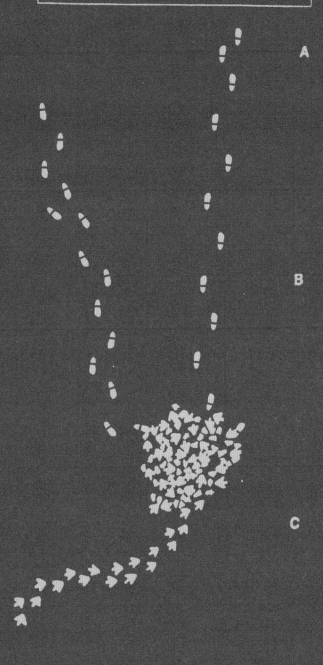

Car Salesman Dad

Ideal Day

It looks like it's just going to be another slow Monday. But Car Salesman Dad knows that just around the corner is the big one, the once-in-a-lifetime moment, the moment when you look up from your desk and through the dealership window and see coming into the yard the kind of car you never see in a used-car lot.

A disheveled pop star, of whom Car Salesman Dad has never heard, wants to sell his 1990 Rolls-Royce Silver Spirit in ocean blue, right now, for cash. In an instant he knows he can buy this car, and he knows someone who might want to buy it from him.

He suggests seven and a half to the pop star, who seems happy with eight, in cash, today. The test drive is sublime and the documentation is all good.

Just around the corner is the big one, the once-in-a-lifetime moment

By midafternoon, Car Salesman Dad has sold the Roller on eBay at a 400 percent markup after he discovered just how famous the pop star actually was. So he's able to knock off early and go to pick the kids up from school. They take the scenic route home and have a celebratory steak dinner.

Car Salesman Dad goes to sleep dreaming of checks and pop stars.

Actual Day

In actuality, Car Salesman Dad sees no one all morning, spending his time polishing and sweeping and such.

Two potential buyers come in at lunchtime. One does nothing but shake his head and kick the vehicles, the other talks too much and it's soon apparent that that's what he wants—to talk.

When the kids get out of school, Car Salesman Dad foolishly gives them some keys so they can sit in the cars and pretend to drive them. He realizes just how foolish this is when he looks up from his desk to see a 1990 Buick Century lurching like a drunken kangaroo across the parking lot. All he can do is watch as it crunches into a low-mileage 2001 Honda Civic automatic.

Nope, no airbags, but did I mention the heavy-duty seatbelts?

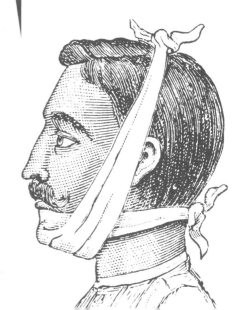

The children are sent home and the rest of the afternoon is spent down at the body shop having the panels beaten back and resprayed.

After dinner and a shower, Car Salesman Dad wants to do some paperwork but is forced to spend the evening flat out on the sofa with bruised ankle, shin, knee, elbow and shoulder watching M*A*S*H reruns with the wife after skidding and destroying his son's toy—an immaculate 1956 Dinky model Rolls-Royce Silver Spirit.

Fashion

You have to have the suits. You can't sell anything without the suits. The suits say confidence and organization and triumph and dreams come true. You can't sell a dream if you're not wearing a suit.

Transport

Car Salesman Dad takes his pick. He's never without an option. As long as it's cars. He doesn't do trains or bikes or taxis, even. He drives.

Snacks

Pastel-colored hard candies from the bowl on his desk. And the always reliable Cup O' Noodles.

Life Expectancy

It's a high-pressure, big stakes game. These things take their toll. Just don't let it be too early. If there's something not quite right with the brakes, get them checked before you borrow the car for a night out with the wife.

Journalist Dad

Ideal Day

A lengthy breakfast while reading the national papers and the international magazines is Journalist Dad's ideal start to the day.

Once the staying in touch is done, the car comes to drive him into town. A few calls from the backseat to confirm the day's arrangements and firm up a few forthcoming assignments and interviews, and there is even time for a quick snooze.

After a light lunch with a moneybags film publicist at the 21 Club, Journalist Dad gets a taxi to the Ritz. His head and chest fill with hubris as he strides toward the desk to announce himself—here to interview Hollywood's goldenest of golden couples for . . . *Vanity Fair*. The golden couple radiate gilt-edged professionalism and all Journalist

Dad has to do is admire their beauty and make sure the tape recorder is working. They happily autograph posters for the kids.

Once the staying in touch is done, the car comes to drive him into town

In the evening, he has a couple of G&Ts at a Soho haunt and a good old brag with a few fellow freelancers, falls asleep on the car ride home, and bursts through the front door just in time to kiss the young ones good night, eat his dinner and fall sleep again in his armchair. Print it.

Actual Day

On a windswept morning in November, as he watches and takes notes on an unimportant game for the local Sunday soccer league, Journalist Dad is almost tempted to question his vocation.

More so when dogged defender Mike "the Bull" Maxwell's sliding tackle continues to slide across the sideline and into him, "completely upending the hapless bystander." At lunch he writes about the game, with a wet pencil on a wet pad, over a warm beer and wet sandwich at the bar.

In the afternoon, he interviews the team's golden couple, the Stotts, who have moved their pig-slaughtering business to town and created 150 jobs, and who must therefore be referred to in only the most glowing of terms. They are boorish and ignorant, and it would take Shakespeare himself to write about them as even vaguely human. He describes them as "charming and erudite" because they don't swear at him.

In the evening, while helping the kids with their homework, Journalist Dad realizes that all three of his children, including his slack-jawed youngest, can spell better than him.

Fashion

If you are the story, as celeb as the celebs you celebrate, you need to dress sharp. White shirts all the time is too newsy. A silk pastel shirt and a quirky tie will get you into features, and into better parties.

If you are not the story, any old suit is okay, but it must be dark because it gets dirty with all the shinning up drainpipes and kneeling in front of mailboxes.

Transport

Journalist Dad has a secondhand car. It is probably a Volkswagen or a Saab. Something quirky is always good, a Fiat 500, perhaps, just in case you get a big scoop and someone wants to make a film about you.

Snacks

Pork scratchings and cigarettes. Cigarettes are snacks, aren't they?

Life Expectancy

There are Journalist Dads and there are Journalist Dads. One might investigate how drunk a wholesome media type gets at parties—he risks a punch on the nose.

Another might be looking into the activities of organized crime in major cities—he risks ending up entombed in a highway flyover. The former is the greater danger but is less often fatal.

I love cigs.

Cop Dad

Ideal Day

The ideal start to Cop Dad's day is being woken up by a 4 a.m. phone call. Here is a dad who likes to hit the ground running.

Lots to mull over back at the station . . .

The streets are good and empty at this time of the day and, in a high-performance unmarked vehicle, he is at the scene in no time. There's a body, a weapon, a footprint and a tire track—lots to mull over back at the station. The footprint and the tire track point to a well-known local bad boy, but the DNA on the weapon suggests someone else.

Cop Dad has to bang his fist on his desk. If he doesn't get to say, "Cuff the toe-rag. I know something you don't know and I'm gonna see you get twenty years for this" by happy hour, someone's going to be sorry.

Cop Dad pulls his tie down a bit, works on a hunch and, after a brief car chase, brings in both the suspects. Sure enough, after a little loud sarcasm and some leaning forward on the desk, they both crack and cry like babies.

When he leaves the bar and goes home, he discovers Cop Mom telling one of the kids off for drawing on the walls. Although too drunk to get involved, Cop Dad amuses himself by shouting "Book 'em, Dano!" before crashing, fully clothed, into bed.

Actual Day

Much of Cop Dad's morning is spent typing up notes and collating evidence and witness statements.

In the afternoon he appears in court. Much of this is sitting around, waiting and drinking gray coffee from a machine, while the case meanders and the judge interrupts. When he does finally get called, he realizes that his pen has leaked in his pocket and green ink has spread across his chest.

All the defense lawyer tries to do is suggest that everything Cop Dad says is a lie, normally a weak strategy, but today it works. The case is thrown out.

Back home, tie down, he eats his dinner from a tray while he watches *CSI*, then finds he's out of cigarettes and beer. In his desperation he resorts to stealing them from his eldest son's room.

When the light goes on, he is caught red-handed by Cop Mom, who then decides that this is the perfect time to sit him down and talk about his drinking problem.

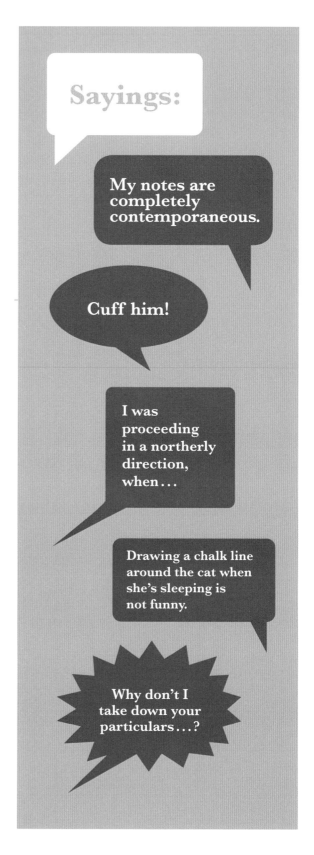

Sayings:

My notes are completely contemporaneous.

Cuff him!

I was proceeding in a northerly direction, when...

Drawing a chalk line around the cat when she's sleeping is not funny.

Why don't I take down your particulars...?

Fashion

Basically you have to get into plain clothes. That's the only way to look good in the force. Who looks cooler—Kojak or Frank Serpico? And, of course, a decent suit for court.

Transport

For work, a souped-up, red but dirty, Vauxhall Cavalier does the business. For the family, a souped-up, red but dirty, Vauxhall Cavalier station wagon does the business.

Snacks

Coffee and doughnuts followed by Nicorette gum and Red Bull. An unstoppable combo.

Life Expectancy

Here is a dad who takes risks, who puts the world to rights and himself on the line. If he gets to retirement, he's got a good pension lined up. Retirement for Cop Dad can be tricky.

His last day on the force is often his most hazardous and he may well find himself being shot. Better to climb the ladder. The life expectancy of a chief of police is higher.

Dangerous Pursuits Dad

Ideal Day

A good way to start the day dangerously is to have slept the night before in a hammock suspended thirty feet up a tree, and to wake with your family around you in their hammocks.

Another reason for this is that Dangerous Pursuits Dad and family are trekking into the Venezuelan forest to find La Mine de Satan, The Devil's Pit. The family is part of a larger party, intent on parachuting into the massive hole.

It is a pretty amazing experience to stand on the precipice above the huge jungle abyss with your four-year-old daughter strapped to your chest. The jump is awesome—straight into darkness, and, when the chute opens, a slow drift down through a cool cave alive with shrieking birds and giant fruit bats.

Dangerous Pursuits Mom follows them down with the toddler.

The seven-hour hike back to the camp is well worth it and tires the kids out

The seven-hour hike back to the camp is well worth it and tires the kids out. By the time they have eaten their barbecued armadillo and sung a few campfire songs, all the family are ready for an early night in the hammocks.

Actual Day

What with it being a Sunday, and Dangerous Pursuits Mom wanting him out of the house so she can repair the zip wire that runs from the parental bedroom to the shed, Dangerous Pursuits Dad takes the kids down to the playground.

The youngsters love the playground because of the extensive monkey bars, and they waste no time monkeying all over them, as surefooted as mountain goats. Dangerous Pursuits Dad has been thinking about the far corner of the climbing frame, which he calls the Old Man's Needle, and reckons that from this point it should be possible to get a couple of ropes across to the top of the slide and climb over without having to touch the ground or step up via the roundabout. It's never been done; nor will it be done today.

While trying to remember what it is Dangerous Pursuits Mom told him to get for lunch on the way home, he misses his footing and falls off the curb. He grazes his knees, shins, elbows and ears, and sprains his ankle. Walking is almost impossible.

Dangerous Pursuits Dad spends the rest of the day on the sofa, watching *Cliffhanger*, while the kids run up the stairs, zip wire down to the shed, run up the stairs again, and so on.

Ouch.

Sayings:

Braced for landing!

I prefer to think of it as *taming* the Zambezi.

Shit happens.

I can't be caged, man!

Fashion

Clothing has to be lightweight and rugged. Accessories are important here: ropes, snap hooks, belt pouches, whistles, emergency flares—all still in their original packaging . . .

Transport

It depends on your pursuit. Mountain bikes, kayaks, four-wheel drives and camels can all be useful. The best way to travel, though, is through the air, by jumping off things.

Snacks

Homemade hammerhead shark jerky and dextrose tablets. All you need.

Life Expectancy

This is not a difficult one. Danger and health do not sit comfortably together. At least it will probably be quick.

Magician Dad

Ideal Day

Breakfast for Magician Dad is in the casino restaurant. Breakfast in Vegas is the breakfast of champions, and ham and eggs, cereal, fresh fruit and pancakes with maple syrup give a busy magician all the powers he needs.

How does he pay for his towering *petit déjeuner*? He passes his hand over the card-swipe machine and smiles at the cashier when it punches out his receipt. Kitchen staff and the gathered throng of customers applaud. Magician Dad takes a bow.

At lunchtime he finds himself opening a supermarket. He turns fruit into vegetable, water into wine and makes a whole line of shopping carts disappear, to the great amusement of the crowd and the fury of the manager.

Back at the casino, for the matinee, he escapes from a padlocked trunk, fixed underwater with a real hippo sitting on it. And for the evening's performance, he chainsaws former supermodel Magician Mom into four pieces and lets his youngest daughter take part in the "spring-loaded spiked-cage trick." The crowd swoons and marvels. The cage trick didn't quite go to plan, but youngest daughter wasn't really hurt and at least she no longer has to ask if she can have her ears pierced.

After much autograph signing and making pens disappear, the family retires to their penthouse suite and changes into their spandex and rhinestone dressing gowns.

Magic!

Actual Day

Magician Dad spends much of the day repairing the box for the sawing-Magician-Mom-in-half trick after the hinge broke last week and Magician Mom screamed out a string of expletives that caused them to be banned from the village hall.

Magician Dad gives his best, but the circumstances are not propitious

At five, after scrambled eggs and toast, the family crams the props and themselves into the Astra and heads off to perform in Nookie Bear's comeback tour.

Magician Dad gives his best, but the circumstances are not propitious. An intern is allowed to operate the lighting and his use of the spotlight means that a number of tricks are not lit—the rabbit emerges from its hat in total darkness, the ripped newspaper reassembles itself in similar stygian gloom.

The sawing-Magician-Mom-in-half routine works, but its success only emphasizes how tiny the audience is, as a smattering of slow single claps and coughs reverberate around the auditorium.

I *so* know how you done that . . .

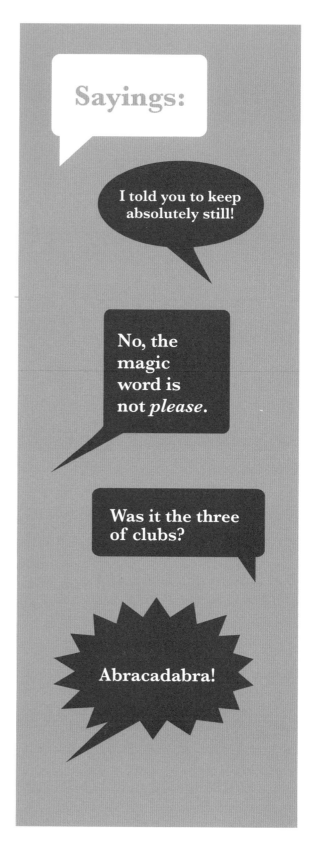

Sayings:

I told you to keep absolutely still!

No, the magic word is not *please*.

Was it the three of clubs?

Abracadabra!

Fashion

The traditional bow tie, top hat and cape are hard to beat. Magicians who wear leather jackets and T-shirts have got it all wrong.

Transport

Flying, obviously. But for starters a specially adapted Volkswagen Beetle with The Great Mysto written on the doors is good.

Snacks

Licorice, and the occasional hard-to-find tropical fruit: guava, jaboticaba or physalis.

Life Expectancy

Magician Dad's life expectancy is pretty good—they're an optimistic sort. The practice of sword-swallowing can significantly affect this.

AVAILABLE FOR WEDDINGS, FUNERALS & BAR MITZVAHS.

"A QUALITY ACT"

THE GREAT MYSTO

Brian—A name synonymous with the color brown. A pipe smoker, a cord wearer and a Volvo driver, Brian is not at home to Mr. Danger, or for that matter Mr. Interesting, Mr. Funny and certainly not Mr. Tickle. Brian scores high on longevity, conformity, stability and low on perversity, sociability and sperm count. In the big scheme of things, Brian just doesn't matter.

Retired Dad

Ideal Day

At 6 a.m. the clock radio comes on. Retired Mom likes Radio 5. Retired Dad goes downstairs and makes coffee to bring back to bed. The couple eats breakfast in the kitchen, sharing toast and jam and bits of the *New York Times*.

In the morning they take the bus down to the golf course and play a round with retired friends. Lunch is a sandwich at the club and then it's off on the bus again to the local bowling alley for a couple of games. Afterward there is time to walk to the shops and stock up on sherry and toffee ice cream.

After an early supper, two daughters-in-law come around with the grandchildren. The little ones crash around, bouncing off the furniture, and, much to Retired Dad's displeasure, eating great canyons through the ice cream tubs. When they leave, after fifteen minutes, he is happy and invigorated, but pleased that the invigoration stops there.

Mom turns off the TV and gives Retired Dad a look

In the evening, Retired Mom watches reruns of *Who Wants to Be a Millionaire?* and *Desperate Housewives*, while Retired Dad sits at his new computer typing up the letters of commendation he received before retirement and researching his family on the Internet.

When the engraved grandfather clock chimes ten, Retired Mom turns off the TV and gives Retired Dad a look.

Actual Day

At just before 6 a.m. Retired Dad is woken by an unfamiliar moaning sound. In the next moment, grandchild number three appears in the doorway and announces that grandchild number two is being sick. Grandchild number three seems unaware that her own face is covered in red spots.

The morning, with the planned bus trip to the club to show the little ones how to play golf now long abandoned, is spent on three different buses getting to the doctor's.

Grandchild number three is sick on bus one; grandchild number two is sick on bus three. On the way home, diagnosis confirmed, immediate containment recommended, grandchild number two is sick on bus one, grandchild number three on bus three.

Despite the fact that Retired Dad tries to leave much of the coping to Retired Mom, the afternoon is spent in a darkened room

reading children's stories, spooning soup, redampening wash cloths and emptying bowls of throw-up. Eventually the patients' proper caregivers turn up from their week away skiing in the Swiss Alps, relieving the shattered Retired Dad and Retired Mom.

Let's try and keep this one off Granddad's shirt . . .

After dinner and a quick sherry or two they collapse into their chairs. Retired Mom gets morose because she doesn't know any of the answers on *Who Wants to Be a Millionaire?* and one of her favorite *Desperate Housewives* characters is killed off.

Sayings:

Better take a coat—it might turn cold.

Take it easy, love.

Bowling is a bit more dynamic than people think.

Sherry?

When the grandfather clock chimes wake them both at ten, Retired Dad realizes that discovering on the Internet that his great-great-grandfather was a famous naval surgeon was just a dream.

Fashion

Just because you are retired there is no reason to let standards slip. A tie and a jacket, ironed slacks, polished shoes and the like—you have to keep it all going. You don't want to start falling apart like your neighbors the Clarks.

Transport

Buses are cheap. What else is there to say?

Snacks

You might think Werther's Originals, but NIPS and Brach's peppermints are surprisingly popular.

Life Expectancy

Technically, of course, Retired Dad could be a multimillionaire in his forties. Probably not, though. Retirement Dad's life expectancy depends on who he was. His territory is too wide. If you have hit retirement, you are already doing pretty good.

Keep it real

New Age Dad

Ideal Day

Before a homemade organic muesli and whole-wheat toast breakfast, there is time to do some yoga and meditation with the kids. The drive to school is beautifully peaceful, as New Age Mom and the kids are all successfully denying the self and listening to the whale song.

The rest of the night is given over to several hours of tantric sex

New Age Dad has a good day at the health-food shop, as several customers are prepared to talk spiritually and holistically when

buying their extra-large tubs of Hi-Performance Glutamine Weight-Gain Capsules. Lunchtime is sunny, and he meditates in the park.

In the evening, after fasting through lunch to gain greater spiritual enlightenment, the kids read out passages from the Bhagavad Gita and New Age Mom practices on Dad for her acupuncture exam.

Once the children are tucked into bed, the rest of the night is given over to several hours of tantric sex.

Actual Day

Everyone oversleeps because the solar-powered alarm clock didn't go off. There is no time for any yoga, which makes New Age Dad feel his age, and the kids use it as an excuse not to make muesli but to have honey-frosted crunchies as an emergency breakfast.

The electricity bill arrives. It is big, and therefore bad in both financial and ecological terms. No one seems able to deny the self on the journey to school and he has to really crank up the whale song to pacify the youngsters.

The only customers at the health-food shop that day are young men with no necks asking if he sells steroids. He tries meditating at lunchtime, but it rains and he can't get the electricity bill out of his mind.

The wild rice and water chestnut dinner is nice, but the kids are getting less prepared to do spiritual readings, preferring instead to lock themselves away and watch sitcoms. New Age Dad's chi is so out of balance that he has to have a Nurofen and half a bottle of Chianti to get rid of his headache.

He takes another Nurofen after New Age Mom has practiced her acupuncture.

Fashion

The main thing is to be comfortable. A Zen state isn't going to come about if your trousers are too tight. Clothing has to be plain. Design and patterning and all that are just going to interfere with the Feng Shui and people's karma. White is good for inner purity, but it stains easily and isn't for work.

Transport

New Age Dad drives a VW camper. Despite all evidence to the contrary, it still seems like the vehicle of the future.

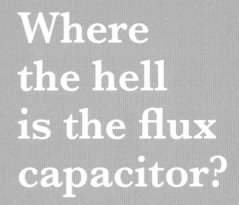

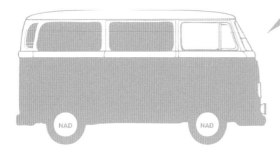

Snacks

Organic macadamia and cashew nuts, four-seed mix with poppy seed sprinkles.

Life Expectancy

A healthy body is a particular concern for this dad, which is always a good sign. However, this is counterbalanced by a preparedness to self-diagnose and eat the bark from some tree rather than visit a doctor.

Rock Dad

Ideal Day

The day begins with Rock Dad putting on his best rock outfit, which Rock Mom has thoughtfully washed and ironed—his tightest-fitting distressed denims and his favorite, worn-but-not-worn-out, Ramones T-shirt.

It's a perfect night out—DC do not disappoint

Much of the working day, down at air traffic control, is spent in a fog of excitement about the evening to come. Once home, and after an energy-providing fry-up and checking the kids all have the right T-shirts on, the whole family piles into the Range Rover and heads for Madison Square Garden to see AC/DC.

It's a perfect night out—DC do not disappoint—and a great opportunity for Rock Dad to show the kids the best ways to pump your fists, play air guitar and get some serious head-banging in.

No one talks on the journey home. They are all too contented and everyone's ears are ringing so much they can't hear one another speak anyway.

Dads still rock. I said, DADS STILL ROCK!

Actual Day

The day begins with Rock Dad realizing that he hasn't put his favorite T-shirt and jeans in the wash. In fact, the only clean trousers available are the brown cords his mother gave him last Christmas.

The fog turns to rain and the family is wet through even before AC/DC appear

The working day is chaotic, as fog has closed JFK and LaGuardia and dozens of aircraft need rerouting. By the time he gets home, he's exhausted.

Because of the fog, driving the Rover up the Long Island Expressway is a nightmare. They arrive late and spend ages trying to park. Once in the auditorium, the fog turns to rain and the family is wet through even before AC/DC appear.

Rock Dad does his best to make the most of things, but the family is forced to leave early when one of the Rock Kids sustains a concussion while head-banging unattended.

Fashion

Denim is obviously important. Two pairs of distressed jeans in rotation is good and either a faded denim jacket or a worn leather biker's jacket will do.

As important as all the denim is a good selection of black T-shirts with band logos and tour dates. The older the dates the better. And some of the T-shirts should be sleeveless. The rock T-shirt is not merely clothing or fashion statement. It's a diary, a souvenir, it's part of who you are.

Transport

Rock Dad used to drive a canary-yellow Ford Capri. But what with marriage and the kids, a Range Rover makes more sense for all sorts of reasons. One day he'll get another Capri.

Snacks

Pepperoni, Snickers bars, After Eights. All housed within glove compartment.

Life Expectancy

There are two main health problems here: tinnitus and the effects of head-banging—neck problems, headaches. Neither is fatal, though quality of life in old age might be affected.

"Woe oh oh oh oh oh. And she's buying a stairway to Heaven."

When I was your age I had eight jobs and five stomach ulcers!

TRY HARDER

Pushy Dad

Ideal Day

On a good day, the kids are up first and doing some homework. A nutritional breakfast sets them up well for the day and it's off to school early enough to get some more practice in before lessons start.

At lunch Pushy Dad nips out of the office to call the kids to discuss that morning's lessons. He takes a full briefcase and leaves the office early so he can run them to their various after-school pursuits.

During the evening meal they discuss how the day went, using the subheadings: Expectations, Goals, Outcomes, Achievement, Progression and the General Plan. The big bonus of the day is that the local paper features all three of his children for their various achievements, two of them pictured.

Even on an ideal day, Pushy Dad has to work late into the night to finish the paperwork he brings home. But it's worth it, as he tiptoes up the stairs in the darkness, to hear one of them crying out from a dreaming sleep, "The only time you'll find success before work is in the dictionary."

Actual Day

The kids are so exhausted that they are difficult to rouse. Even repeating the Five Statements for a Successful Day fails to get them going.

They arrive at school early enough for practice, but he sees them scuttle to the far side of the playground, where they stand around text-messaging. When he tries to call them at lunch for a progress report, they are unavailable.

In the afternoon an important meeting is extended and the kids have to get the bus to practice. Pushy Dad feels the loss of an opportunity to discuss the day's physics lesson with his son.

When he finally gets home there is much debate about how the kids managed to miss the bus to practice. During the evening meal no one wants to talk and he feels the vast abyss of disappointment opening beneath him.

As he climbs the dark stairs to bed, he counts off the Five Statements for a Successful Day, realizing that none of them has been realized.

Fashion

The Pushy Dad isn't really concerned about fashion. You need a suit for awards ceremonies, but that's about it.

Transport

The Volvo 240 is what you need. Rugged and reliable and plenty of space for sports kits, double basses, etc.

Snacks

Lindt white chocolate truffles.

Life Expectancy

The truth is that the life expectancy of the Pushy Dad can be affected by stress. Still, death tends not to come until (but soon after) he has witnessed his progeny's great achievement. Sometimes on TV, from his deathbed.

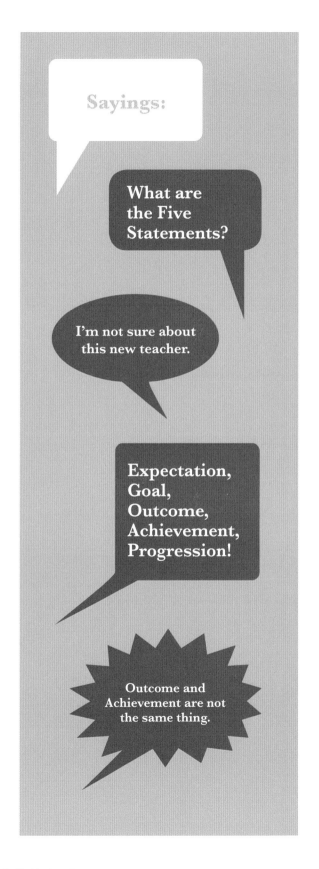

Sayings:

What are the Five Statements?

I'm not sure about this new teacher.

Expectation, Goal, Outcome, Achievement, Progression!

Outcome and Achievement are not the same thing.

$$D^2 = \frac{1}{C}\frac{1}{\ell}\frac{d\ell}{dt} = \frac{1}{C}\frac{1}{P}\frac{dP}{dt} \qquad OPC =$$

$$A^2 = \frac{1}{P^2}\frac{P_0 - P}{P} \sim \frac{1}{53} = (GUARDIAN)^{(1a)}$$

$$D^2 \frac{K\varrho}{3} + \bigcirc + \square^2 = (2a)$$

Teacher Dad

Ideal Day

Of course teaching is a vocation and he's never "off duty." Equally the ideal day for Teacher Dad is one of his many holidays.

After a burger-and-fries supper, the family goes to see the new Pedro Almodóvar film

So, after a breakfast at the B&B, they head down to the beach. Teacher Mom and Teacher Dad can sit in deck chairs and read the *Post* and *New York Times* respectively, while keeping an eye on the young ones' unstructured learning time. They are

building a sandcastle. Their construction does credit to their scholarly upbringing.

They are able to draw on a variety of fields of learning and combine them effectively in a clearly defined system of interrelations. Meaning that the boy builds a minireservoir to solve the drainage problem with his moat, while the girl opts for some gothic castellation because it would "attract chivalrous knights."

After a burger-and-fries supper, the family goes to see the new Pedro Almodóvar film. On the walk home the kids discuss the film with just a little prompting from Teacher Dad.

They all go to bed tired, happy and having learned something.

Actual Day

An actual day, though, naturally, is spent working. Much of that working is managing OPC—other people's children. And other people's children are a bum bunch.

As he stares out of the window while the pupils work their way through the first five equations on page 22 before checking the working out with a neighbor, or while they score their names into the desks with penknives and shoot holes in the curtains with air pistols, Teacher Dad does some math of his own—years, months, weeks, days, hours, minutes and seconds to retirement.

He has to stay behind for parents' evening. The cafeteria has laid on a slab of cheeselike material and a radish on a paper plate covered with plastic wrap. The parents are distraught, resigned, accusatory, bewildered, indifferent and insane in equal measure.

He corrects homework and eats a sandwich

By the time he gets home the kids are in bed. He corrects homework and eats a sandwich. Teacher Mom goes to bed too. He joins her once he's prepared tomorrow's lunches and packed the kids' bags.

He finds a penknife in his son's backpack, which sends him to bed tired, unhappy and afraid he's learned something.

Sayings:

The first five questions on page 22.

I read it in the *Times.*

What does that tell us?

Be quiet!

Fashion

A couple of years in, Teacher Dad finds himself settling into cardigans and corduroy jackets with leather elbow patches. After all, they're just kids, how stylish do you have to be? And as he gets on in years he can really let himself go. No one will care.

Transport

For the trip to work, the bicycle. If it's raining very hard, Teacher Mom can drop him off in the wagon.

Snacks

Doughnuts and muffins in the faculty lounge, week-old birthday cake, four mini Bounty bars left over from the last fund-raiser.

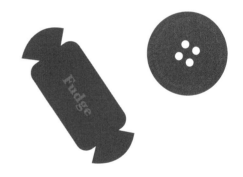

Life Expectancy

Because of all the stresses and strains of "the lifestyle," it can go two ways: either you've built up the stamina and can go on for decades or you crack up on retirement.

The punters like it when I model the antique clobber, innit.

Antiques Dealer Dad

Ideal Day

With the kids on vacation comes the chance for a good day's antiquing *en famille*. The family hits the road early, taking BLT sandwiches and iced tea in the car and setting off for the countryside.

On arrival at a likely-looking old town, Antiques Dealer Dad checks out the local auction viewing, while the kids and the missus shop and drink coffee. They rendez-vous back at the vehicle for their packed lunch and to discuss who bids for what. The trick is not to let the locals catch on to what you might have spotted. The stakes are high.

Dad has spotted an eighteenth-century bookcase, needs work obviously, but it could be a total bargain. Eldest son will bid for this. For eldest daughter, a painted jug, definitely nineteenth-century, totally without chips.

Youngest child and Antiques Dealer Mom will bid for a nice early 1900s French cigar case.

The trick is not to let the locals catch on to what you might have spotted

The plan works beautifully, even when he bids against his own son twice so that he could shake his head dramatically the third time. Everything gets bundled into the Volvo and, on the journey home, there is much singing and laughing and calculating of markups.

Actual Day

The day starts with the trek to the country. Today there are three auctions simultaneously, so the family has to split up, which means that the children are not to bid on anything they find without consulting Antiques Dealer Dad first.

Dad had already got into a stupid macho bidding contest with a local dealer who spilled his wife's thermos

What this means in practice is that the kids never reappear, and when they are collected they have with them some Nazi memorabilia—daggers, cap badges, SS armbands and the like, seven Edwardian dolls in various stages of decay, and what was sold as the fossil of an early shrewlike mammal but is quite clearly only painted on to the rock.

And dad had already got into a stupid macho bidding contest with a local dealer who spilled his wife's thermos. The result of which was his paying well over the asking price for a bit of Spode. The journey home is spent silently calculating the cost.

I feel old.

Sayings:

Hmm, it looks old, but is it?

I'll bring the Volvo around.

That's what I call a markup.

Definitely eighteenth century.

Fashion

You do have to look the part. You are selling, wheeling and dealing with class and the past. So you have to look a bit behind the times and a bit like a dandy.

The ideal combination is brown wing tips, fawn-colored corduroy pants, a green, fine-knit lamb's wool crewneck sweater and a yellow silk cravat. Outdoors, add a Barbour jacket and a tweed flat cap. Suits and ties are for art dealers.

Transport

The Volvo wagon is without equal in the eyes of the antiques community. Antiques Dealer Dad would only be letting himself down if he drove anything else. It's rare to find a piece of furniture you can't get in the back.

Snacks

Ghirardelli. Green & Black's 85% Dark. Altoid mints in emergencies.

Life Expectancy

The thing about all that fancy stuff—the furniture and paintings, the lamps, the jewels, the commodes—is that it encourages ideas of grandeur. Antiques Dealer Dad can be a bit red of cheek if he's not careful.

He does tend to live at least until he has seen the ordinary and average from his own childhood become desirable and collectible and highly valuable.

Objection, baby!

Lawyer Dad

Ideal Day

Wednesday, 10 a.m. Supreme Court.

Lawyer Dad listens to the sensuous sliding sound of his silk as he reaches forward to undo the spring-loaded catches of his black leather Tumi briefcase and take out his files.

Today is a day of great, table-turning drama. Today is the day that will change the course of this trial definitively. He is the only one who knows this. People's lives are in his hands. He is going to use his intellectual powers to see that the cause of justice is furthered, to show the gallery, press and public, that the truth, should sufficient funds be forthcoming, will out.

After a few minor points with a minor witness, beautifully lulling all assembled

into a state of mild torpor, Lawyer Dad surveys his stage, smiles jovially and calls for witness X. A brief hubbub circles the room, dissipating with the arrival of the

He hears the rustle of the silk once more...

surprise witness. With the right coaxing and encouragement, witness X's testimony electrifies the gallery, the jury, the judge and the defense team.

As witness X leaves the witness box, still wiping tears from her eyes, the accused looks defeated, the jury looks deeply moved, nodding at one another, and the judge gives

Lawyer Dad a brief but significant glance. He hears the rustle of the silk once more.

He might even be home in time for a game of softball in the yard with children A and B.

Actual Day

Thursday, 4:30 p.m. Franklin County Municipal Court.

Lawyer Dad, after finally managing to undo the stupid catch on the briefcase he bought at a garage sale, reaches in to take out his brief. He shouldn't be here. He is standing in for a sick colleague.

It takes him several minutes to realize he's looking at the wrong files and he has to resort to spilling his case and the paperwork onto the floor in order to get the right file without looking as though he's a total fool. The other lawyer and the judge look suspicious.

The claimant—his dog dug up my flower beds and urinated on a child's bike—is not pleased to be represented by a stranger and the proceedings descend into an argument between two feuding neighbors.

When the judge wades in with his judgment just to get the shouters to shout no more, he reserves a little segment of his conclusion to give Lawyer Dad a ticking off for his inept performance.

When he goes home, the horticultural dog owner tries to attack him and he has to lock himself in his car to avoid a bashing. At home he sits in his chair and prepares his papers for the next day, while Lawyer Mom and the kids watch reruns of *L.A. Law* on TV.

When all the family is in bed, he lays down his paperwork, gets out the *The Firm* video and goes to sleep dreaming he's Mitch McDeere.

> **Small service is true service, while it lasts.**

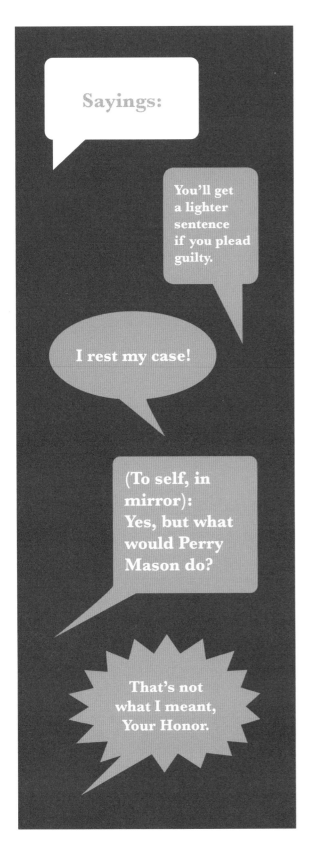

Sayings:

You'll get a lighter sentence if you plead guilty.

I rest my case!

(To self, in mirror): Yes, but what would Perry Mason do?

That's not what I meant, Your Honor.

Fashion

Lawyer Dad aspires to one of the crazier fashion anachronisms. In sartorial terms, he harkens back to the seventeenth century. He likes wigs and gowns, pantaloons, black socks, big-buckled shoes. He's a role player.

Transport

It's okay to start with a bicycle, but it should be taxis eventually. And a nice big German car for days out *en famille*.

Snacks

Bags of chips and stale candy bars from the vending machine.

Life Expectancy

Life expectancy is good. Very few are the Lawyer Dads who have been murdered by a client. The best possible health care is available once the hospital realizes what Lawyer Dad is.

You can't handle the truth!

Army Dad

Ideal Day

Reveille is at **0630 hours**.

Cleaning and polishing till **0700 hours**, then breakfast.

Inspection at **0800**.

Aboard the vehicle at **0810 hours**.

At **0835 hours** disembark at school.

Proceed to work.

0850–1745 hours, work.

Arrive home **1800 hours**.

1800–1830 hours, watch news.

1830–1900 hours, school debriefing.

Dinner from **1900–1930**; children homework.

Adults washing up from **1930 hours**.

2045 hours, children's bath.

2130 hours, children to bed, adults cleaning, ironing, preparing for next day.

2230 hours, parents to bed.

Veni, vidi, daddy.

Actual Day

Reveille is at **0630 hours** and again at **0640** and again at **0642**.

Cleaning and polishing till **0646 hours**, then breakfast.

Inspection at **0800** and then again at **0810**.

Aboard the vehicle at **0825 hours**.

0857 hours disembark at school. Proceed to work. Arrive late.

0915–1845 hours, work.
Arrive home **1900 hours**.

1903–1931 hours, school debriefing.

1932–1944 hours, parental reprimand in response to poor school debriefing.

Dinner from **1945–2003**; children homework.

Adults washing up from **2003 hours.**

2137 hours, children's bath.

2214 hours, children to bed, adults cleaning, ironing, preparing for next day.

2338 hours, parents to bed.

2339–0009 hours, indigestion.

Sayings:

> Pays to be a winner, now back you go again, sir.

> Put that light out!

> Damn you! Goddamn you! Nobody D.O.R.'s after eleven weeks! Nobody!

> The chain of command is there for a very good reason, young lady.

Fashion

Khaki. What else is there?

Transport

When the chips are down, only a Land Rover will give you the flexibility and toughness you need.

Snacks

Mars bar. You can sing the song from the ad while you march.

Life Expectancy

The life expectancy of an Army Dad depends on how often he is on active service. In recent years life expectancy has declined a little.

> Oh, brother, I think I pulled my back again.

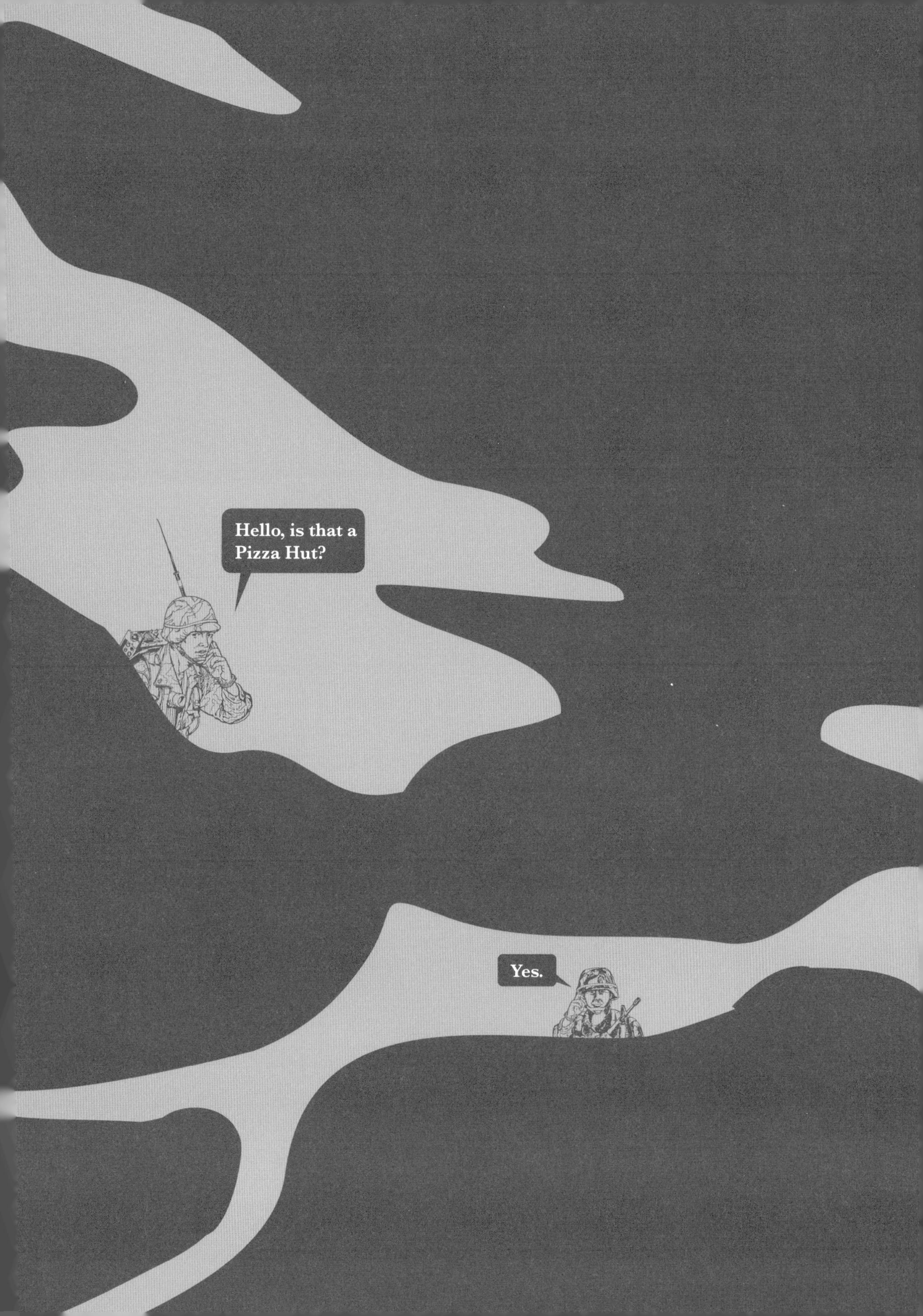
Hello, is that a Pizza Hut?
Yes.

So I says to the geezer, "No, Humphrey, that just won't do."

Gangster Dad

Ideal Day

Up early, Gangster Dad has fruit juice, cereal, coffee and a cigar for breakfast. Five minutes polishing the car and he's off. Not much crime happens before lunch, so a round of golf with some cronies is always a good bet.

Gangster Dad collects his son's lunch money

Lunch is an unhealthily large sandwich and a couple of beers at the bar for a bit of gossip and a few wisecracks. When the kids get home from school, Gangster Dad collects his son's lunch money. Their arrangement is not that the youngster gets lunch money from his father, but that he gets it from other pupils and gives his old man a cut. It's been a good day and father and son both get a feeling of warmth as they divvy out the takings.

After a big family dinner with Mom and Grandma and Uncle Steve and Auntie Kelly and Cousin Gavin and all seven of Gangster Dad's kids, they settle down en masse to watch the wide-screen version of *Godfather II* on a recently acquired 60-inch flat-screen Sony with six-speaker surround sound and subwoofer.

It's great to sit with the whole family and stare speechlessly at deified machismo and violence. It's a real shared experience. Gangster Dad drinks lots of beer and falls asleep in his armchair, a sleeping child on each leather-upholstered arm.

Actual Day

An early breakfast followed by coffee and a cigar while reading the papers is not a bad start to the day. Unless the breakfast was stale Shredded Wheat with tepid milk, the coffee from a vast vat made some hours previously. After five minutes of smoking the la-di-da there is so much thick blue smoke in the cell that reading the paper, even if it is yesterday's, is next to impossible.

The best thing to do is go for a brisk walk. This Gangster Dad does, after waiting for two hours. He walks in a circle, usually doing between twenty-three and twenty-six circuits, depending on how respected he is feeling.

After a disappointing lunch, he does the rounds of the TV and table-tennis rooms, being respected and giving out advice to other prisoners about things like respect. For an hour he is allowed to work outside in the allotment, where he and Terry "the Lobster" Tucker discuss their plans for breakout.

After a lackluster dinner he goes back to his cell to lie on his bunk and read his mail. With Dad away, his son's lunch-money racket is meeting some resistance.

While the rest of the prisoners are watching *Godfather II* on a 14-inch Kenwood, Gangster Dad is trying to figure out how quickly he can get a message to Gangster Mom that she's going to need to be a little more involved in the family side of things while dad is elsewhere. At least she knows where the guns are. Game girl!

Sayings:

I'm just breaking your balls, Warden.

I don't know nothing. Maybe he just left town for a while.

Are you cracking wise with me? Now go to bed.

It should work. It's just out of the box.

Fashion

A sharp suit is good, or a new leather jacket with a crewneck underneath. Gold rings and chains are must-have accessories. No sneakers, you muppet.

Transport

The only way to travel is in luxury and style. Quite what these words mean is debatable. The best guide is newest and latest. And big, you need big. A Jag or one of those Range Rovers. Plenty of leather interior.

Snacks

Either prosciutto sandwiches or mozzarella balls and artichoke hearts. Or the rock-hard Marathon bar from the canteen.

Life Expectancy

Ask yourself. It's not hard. Yes, some Gangster Dads get to an impressive age and then keel over in their vineyards from natural causes. Plenty don't.

Artist Dad

Ideal Day

During the morning Artist Dad finally gets the right shade for the thatched roofs in the top right-hand corner of the canvas.

He also decides that dropping cigarette ash on the foreground has turned out not to be a disaster, as he first thought, but one of life's beneficial accidents, as it lends the dry-stone wall and the gravel a certain extra quality.

Lunch is artisan fare—bread, cheese and red wine in the company of friendly but slightly less successful painters. The afternoon is spent asleep on the sofa.

After dinner is spent potato-printing with the kids. And talking to them about perspective and the Renaissance.

Actual Day

During the morning Artist Dad messes up the color of the thatched roofs in the top right-hand corner of the painting. He realizes that not only did he drop cigarette ash on the picture, he actually burned a hole in the canvas.

The afternoon is spent asleep on the sofa, dreaming of a color he just can't seem to make on the palette

He gives up and goes to the bar, but no one shows up. The afternoon is spent asleep on the sofa, dreaming of a color he just can't seem to make on the palette.

After dinner, while potato-printing with the kids, Artist Dad realizes that his four-year-old is printing triangles of exactly the right shade for the roofs on the ruined canvas.

Sayings:

I'm painting light itself!

One day they'll understand.

Mostly I'm saying something about form and content.

Who burned a hole in this canvas?

Fashion

Traditional Artist Dad may still go for the smock, though neckerchiefs and berets don't really work nowadays. Certainly the hands-on Artist Dad will wear some sort of paint-spattered overalls much of the time.

Modern Artist Dad may just wear a black turtleneck and a designer suit. There's no need to get grubby if you're exhibiting a couple of new video installations.

Transport

Generally the bus. Taxis if it's to a gallery. When success finally arrives, a nice quirky red sports car.

Snacks

Olives, crusty bread, goat cheese salad. Simple fare. A palette, with possibilities for composition. Beer and wine are sort of snacks.

Life Expectancy

This depends on whether the dad is unusually abstemious or the type to go through forty Gauloise and a bottle of whiskey most days. Artists, if consumption, pneumonia, suicide, murder at the hands of a jealous lover, etc., don't get them, have good natural life expectancy. Why? The old "lust for life" syndrome.

Trouble is—that's what leads to the Gauloise-and-whiskey lifestyle.

Inventor Dad

Ideal Day

The sun is shining, the birds are singing in the trees and the only place to be is in the shed.

The hours spent working on the new flanges have paid off, and they turn out to be a precision piece of home engineering. The formula for the advanced polymer, unstable though it might have been for a while, looks like it might work at last. But the headline-grabber will surely be the successful development of the luminous lab coat, an idea so simple, so useful, so eco-friendly, that all the world will want it.

Inventor Dad comes back to the house beaming and glowing with self-belief and success. At dinner he makes the kids roar with laughter because he says things like, "If you don't eat your broccoli I know a pro-particle sema-bot that will!"

Inventor Mom knows that dad is off to the Patent Office in the morning and they celebrate by firing up the newly completed Hypergasmofoggatronic.

Actual Day

The sleet is falling for a fifth consecutive day and an icy wind is piercing every crack in the shed's aging woodwork. Water has dripped from the roof onto the stage-four plans and the measurements are illegible.

The flanges are missing and the cat has eaten the new polymer, a highly unstable compound, and is stuck to the door. To top it all off, the luminous lab coat, which seemed so promising, has hit a problem. Working with it in the shed seems to be giving Inventor Dad one heck of a tan.

When he goes back to the house he is cold, wet and despondent but glowing nonetheless. Inventor Mom tells him he'll soon be on the cover of *OK!* magazine just by dint of his extreme orangeness.

He doesn't say much over dinner and all the family knows that tomorrow is not a Patent Office day. Tomorrow is a shed day.

Fashion

For inventing there is a choice—either the lab coat, bought as a student, but still perfectly serviceable; or there is the boiler suit, bought for that first job at ICI all those years ago. Inventor Dad does have a suit. It's brown, and there's a brown tie to go with it. The suit is worn for trips to the Patent Office.

Transport

The bicycle. It's still a magnificent machine and a superb means of maintaining fitness. The train for trips to the Patent Office.

Snacks

Jawbreakers, suckers, Certs Wintergreen mints. Anything that will last through those long hours in the shed.

Life Expectancy

Inventor Dads can go on for years. They are curious, optimistic and tenacious. Just the qualities needed for a damn good inning. A minority are lost to explosions, electrocution, radiation poisoning or madness, but, on the whole, the odds are good.

Sayings:

Eureka!

Oh, bother

All it needs is a few minor adjustments.

My hand is definitely on fire!

PART
THREE

D

Dads Through the Ages

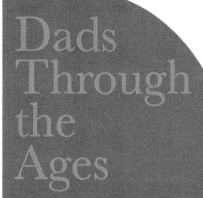

Dads Through the Ages

Modern Dad doesn't know he's born. So says Postwar Generation Dad. And, of course, in some ways this is merely another familiar remark in the generational conversation that has been going as long as dads themselves. But Modern Dad really does maintain a strikingly privileged position in comparison to his historical counterparts. Modern Dad has parental powers undreamed of by his forebears. Things like Disney videos and Nickelodeon. But it wasn't always so.

I really must fire my stylist!

Neanderthal Dad

While Neanderthal Dad may not have had Xboxes, My Little Pony or even school to divert the children, the pace of life was slower and the children less demanding. But with no school, it falls to Dad to make sure the youngsters learn how to make spears and stone axes, how to kill and skin animals, how to make fire, how to defend your cave from wolves and bears. So there's always something to do.

Neanderthal Dad takes the free-range approach to parenting. Without the threat of social services, the kids are allowed to roam wild in the ample backyard. Until hunting time that is, when they can come in handy in baiting the saber-toothed tigers and other beasts. Neanderthal Mom might not approve, but a few aggrieved grunts is easy enough to ignore.

What really keeps Neanderthal Dad and his large brain warm at night is his big idea. The big idea is for his daughter, who is not at all bad looking for an early proto-human, to get together with one of those new Cro-Magnon men. They're one heck of a sophisticated bunch.

Without the threat of social services, the kids are allowed to roam wild in the ample backyard

Mythic Hero Dad

With Mythic Hero Dad anything can happen. But whatever does happen, it's sure to be an adventure.

School isn't really an issue when you're out for the day challenging demigods

No, never a dull moment for this dad's kids. School isn't really an issue when you're out for the day challenging demigods or fighting off minotaurs, harpies and sirens.

Besides, dad's too busy taking care of business himself to worry too much about what the kids are up to. He's got enough on his plate with appeasing tyrant kings, bare ankle shooting and cleaning out stinky stables. Sometimes, there just aren't enough hours in the day.

If the children do go off to work with dad, they won't be seeing too much of mom. She's staying at home and being the epitome of fidelity and faith. She needn't worry, though, because the kids will be regularly tested and learn in their own fashion. Quests and trials are not unlike coursework and exams.

We are the Romans!

Roman Dad

Why should Roman Dad need Prozac or Ritalin to keep his children in check? He has gladiatorial combat, chariot races and lions eating Christians to keep them attentive and off the streets.

There's so much to do with them and no social workers telling you that you can't

It's a free for all! Ancient Rome is a great place to bring up children. There's so much to do with them and no social workers telling you that you can't.

Roman Dad does, of course, have a few of those universal dad problems—once they're teenagers, the kids can be moody and a bit rude to the slaves, having them put to death for trivial reasons and so on.

Then there are the phases—teenage daughter wanting to join the Vestal Virgins. Roman Dad and Roman Mom are quick to point out what this will mean in terms of orgy invitations. But she won't be told. And the son wants to be a legionnaire and work in Britain. He says the landscape and climate make Tuscany look drab.

It could be worse—at least they don't want to go into politics, or marry each other.

Darn, it's stuck again.

Viking Invasion Dad

If your dad is a Viking invader, you might have to accept a lot of brothers and sisters with mothers who aren't yours. Though if you're in the real family, back home in Denmark, you probably won't get to meet them.

In fact family life in general is somewhat unorthodox, as Viking Dad is away a lot, sometimes for several years at a stretch. But if and when he returns, you'll get as many solid gold presents as any child could wish for: bangles, hair clips, brooches, necklaces—the classic pillaged booty.

Back at the homestead, Viking Dad's not one to relax. There are plenty of local knockarounds to get stuck into and there's always an axe that needs smithing or a local village that needs plundering.

A good Viking Mom understands Viking Dad's need to let off steam down at the meadhall with the boys after a hard day's plundering, but she's always insistent the kids be taught the tools of the trade.

If he's feeling generous, he might let you wear the hat with the upturned horns and see it as his personal duty to show you how to make a man you've just killed into the famous "blood eagle."

Crusades Dad

This dad gives the young 'uns one heck of a religious spirit.

There are not many other children who can say they took part in the biggest, longest and bloodiest religious war. After marching across Europe to defend the Holy Land, the little ones can get quite tired. Fortunately Crusades Dad keeps the bedtime stories short—only a verse or two of his favorite Bible passages.

But the long walks and lulls between bloodshed can leave youngsters bored, so it's up to Crusades Dad to teach them the tenets behind all these fights.

With Crusades Mom home running the house and servants, it's up to Crusades Dad to keep the kids in line and out of trouble. And, if they make it to Jerusalem, it's a fantastic day of conquering and learning!

Father, it's worse than I feared. I think it could be *Man Flu*.

Black Death Dad

Sometimes it's hard to be a dad.

When your village, county and country are afflicted with plague is one such time. And it looks as if letting the children keep rats as pets was a bad idea too.

Black Death Dad knows how challenging parenting can be

The whole year and a half that the local population were sprouting buboes, turning black and dropping dead while you talked to them was a tricky time to be a parent.

It certainly wasn't easy after Black Death Mom bought the big one, leaving Black Death Dad as a single parent. Despite his attempts to get back out there, the dating scene's been a bit quiet of late. Whatever healthy women are left always have a throng of hopeful men lining up around the block.

It's not easy grounding your kids for eighteen months. They get stir-crazy. The broken spinning wheel and the key ring with one key on it get boring quickly. Having to lock one out of the house when the boils appear is even harder.

Black Death Dad knows how challenging parenting can be.

Machiavellian Dad

Life can be a bit grim if you can't trust your father. And Machiavellian Dad instills this distrust into his children by means of manipulation, betrayal and, in extreme circumstances, torture.

The kids get to have the coolest last name in the class

Much of the time, though, he's great fun, and sees that the family makes the most of court life. After all, those Borgias can be a real laugh sometimes. And the kids get to have the coolest last name in the class.

On the other hand, life isn't all that sweet for Machiavellian Mom. If it's not the endless power lunches with other ambitious couples, then it's Machiavellian Dad's fork-tongued sweet talking that means he's always wangling his way out of the dish washing.

But never forget: in his thinking, this Dad is suspended over a pit of infinite despair and meaninglessness, where fleeting power is the only thing of any worth. Not a good place for a dad to be.

Shlurrrrrrrrrrp!

Eighteenth-Century Scientist Dad

The kitchen, the front room, the hallway and the downstairs bathroom are all filled with bubbling glass flasks and tubes and clamps and burners and more tubes. Eighteenth-Century Scientist Dad is attempting to produce a gas hitherto undiscovered by man.

So when one of them is blown out through the kitchen window and into a nearby forest, it isn't anybody's fault

Eighteenth-Century Scientist Mom has taken most of the twelve children to her mother's so she can write her feminist tract. But two have absconded and are running along the hall throwing vials of acid at each other.

These two children are dearly loved by their father; of this there can be no doubt. But when an experiment is in progress, Dad has to maintain his high state of concentration and cannot be expected to consider all eventualities. So when one of them is blown out through the kitchen window and into a nearby forest, it isn't anybody's fault and nobody thinks any the worse of him.

Things were different then. That's why you had twelve children.

Graham

Graham—With a tendency to laugh at
inappropriate moments during films, Graham
is a slow-moving, big, round bear of a man who
nevertheless enjoys the full range of North Face
clothing and always carries a compass or Swiss
Army knife. Unable to successfully reverse a car
down even the widest street, his greatest fear is
driving in Arches National Park.

Merde!

Off with his head!

French Revolution Dad

Life with French Revolution Dad starts off as a real blast.

What great "family time" they've spent hating the aristocracy and watching their beheadings

The kids have begun their lives as grumbling peasants with no hope for any improvement in their existence. So to take part, with dad, in the storming of the Bastille is an exhilarating experience.

Then there's the sitting around in coffee shops discussing politics with dad and his cronies and the excitement at the unveiling of the Declaration of the Rights of Man. Meanwhile, French Revolution Mom can't stop telling her story about the march on Versailles. And all that cake to eat as well. Yummy. Will the fun never cease?

And what great "family time" they've spent hating the aristocracy and watching their beheadings.

But, in the end, the pressure to defame and denounce is irresistible. When the kids eventually turn dad over to the authorities, the family has finally done its bit in acting as a vague metaphor for the revolution.

Puritan Dad

For the children of Puritan Dad, there is an upside and a downside.

The upside is that you probably get to go to heaven, if that's your cup of tea. The downside is that for your time here on earth dad is going to make sure that you behave yourself.

It's not so much the incessant itching or the nonstop preaching, it's the fact that however nice the girlfriend or boyfriend you take home, Puritan Dad isn't going to accept them until there's a ring on your finger. This old man's no easy touch.

His brood are fitted for hair shirts at an early age. Their lives are pretty austere and they can expect to spend quite a bit of time in church and/or reading the Bible. At least they'll never be lost for a pithy proverb.

Puritan Dad's intensity makes him hard to love and live up to, and his fixations with sin and the flesh make him a bit boring. He's certainly not the one to turn to when you need sex education.

His fixations with sin and the flesh make him a bit boring

Industrial Revolution Dad

One great invention is all that Industrial Revolution Dad needs. But no matter how hard he works, and how much of his wife's inheritance he squanders on washers and soldering irons, it just doesn't seem to work out:

- The sheep-operated shearing machine was a failure.

- The engine powered by gravity never got off the ground.

- The microscope oven was a commercial flop.

The missus has had it up to her eyes with the sulphurous smells and the constant cries of "Darling, I've seen the future and it's egg-shaped!" and has her heart set on a steadier, less topsy-turvy life.

If he gets it right, his invention will change people's lives and speed economic progress. But, in the meantime, at least he's got children to send out to work if money for the inventing runs short.

"Darling, I've seen the future and it's egg-shaped!"

Argh, wanna buy a Cuban?

Smuggler Dad

You know the saying—"A Smuggler Dad raises a wily child."

It's true. Smuggler Dad is all about a sort of coastal version of "the knowledge."

Smuggler Dad's belle is wide of waist and short of teeth, and is as crooked as she is whiffy. As with her husband, she has a suspiciously good grasp of many European languages and incredible night vision, can drink many a man under the table and provide ballast for a dinghy full of whiskey barrels. What a woman.

The caves, the passageways, the hideouts. This is the wisdom he passes on to his youngsters. That, and a total disregard for the law and a general suspicion toward anyone from outside the village.

Smuggler Dad's child drinks only rum and smokes only Cubans. Poor but happy. And often drunk and with a nasty cough.

Smuggler Dad is all about a sort of coastal version of "the knowledge"

Rawhide!

Wild West Dad

Wild West Dad falls into two camps—Sheriff Dad and Outlaw Dad.

Sheriff Dad will make sure you can shoot straight and handle yourself in a confrontation with rustlers

Sheriff Dad is a pretty important parent, what with being a Dad *and* upholding the law *and* keeping Outlaw Dad out of town. Sheriff Dad and Outlaw Dad are, of course, mirror images of each other, and their fates are likewise entwined.

Sooner or later they will end up meeting each other in a showdown. All bets are off as to the victor, but if Sheriff Dad has a cleft chin and a macho swagger, he's pretty much a shoo-in.

As parents, both will be aware of the presence of guns around their children.

Outlaw Dad would be more likely to let you take a gun to Outlaw camp and teach you how to mount a horse quickly when leaving a saloon in a hurry, for example. But he's also more likely to shoot at you in a drunken funk.

Sheriff Dad will make sure you can shoot straight and handle yourself in a confrontation with rustlers. And, despite being fancied by the town's best-looking madam, he'll never leave mom. He's not that type of guy.

Trench Foot Dad

A postcard arrives home. It is from Trench Foot Dad. It is dated July 21, 1916. The kids are all excited and want to hear it read again and again.

It's a shame that when he's home on leave all his son wants to know is how many Germans he's killed

It doesn't say much. The most important thing it says is that he is alive. That he has survived the worst single day in the history of the U.S. Army.

The children don't understand why the postcard makes their mother cry, but they remember deeply that it does.

Trench Foot Dad has to fight in some of the worst conditions imaginable, but being away from his wife and children still manages to be additional suffering. It's a shame that when he's home on leave all his son wants to know is how many Germans he's killed.

It doesn't matter, though. Children are children.

It's comforting for the man sitting in a building for the first time in three months. What he hopes is that his own children aren't caught up in global conflagration twenty years down the road.

No, it doesn't seem possible.

Nothing to see here, Officer...

Speakeasy Dad

If you are running a grubby, subterranean, smoke-filled, illegal drinking den, having kids around is useful, and caters for a more family-oriented clientele.

Speakeasy Dad just has to be careful that his children don't develop a taste for hooch at too early an age

They can meet guests, collect and clean glasses, empty ashtrays, change barrels and keep an eye out for the odd law-upholding flatfoot. They're also great for cleaning those hard-to-reach nooks and crannies that Speakeasy Dad doesn't have the patience for.

It's educational for them to meet and talk to all sorts of criminal types and start deciding which of the Big 3—crooked bookie, numbers man, moonshine runner—they'd like to become. They feel secure because dad is behind the bar talking to the local chief of police and the mayor, and proud because of the couple of floozies hanging off the old man's arms.

Speakeasy Dad just has to be careful that his children don't develop a taste for hooch at too early an age, get blown up in brewing explosions and that they don't get flipped and rat him out to the feds.

This is White Rabbit. Can I come in from the cold? Over...

Cold War Spy Dad

Meetings with Cold War Spy Dad can take place in safe houses only. He always runs the shower and stands at the curtain looking out when he talks to you.

Cold War Spy Dad one day suddenly appears at the front door with a new nose...

Christmas and birthday presents have to be collected from drop boxes, or swapped for identical Christmas and birthday presents on a park bench. At such meetings Cold War Spy Dad doesn't make eye contact, and will likely be chain-smoking an imported brand of cigarette.

And when he phones it's usually from a call box in what he still insists on calling West Germany.

He is a mysterious but righteous and lovable dad, with a penchant for tan Macintoshes and wispy mustaches.

When one day he doesn't come back, it's hard for the youngsters and for Cold War Spy Mom, until twenty years later when Cold War Spy Dad one day suddenly appears at the front door with a new nose, an Omar Sharif mustache and going by the name of Yuri Dunfogiev.

One small step
for Dad...
One giant leap
for Dadkind...

Space Dad

All the children are jealous of Space Dad's kids. He's so rare. He's like a highly collectable Dungeons & Dragons figure, which makes him a tough act to follow.

Space Dad always wants his food in small, freeze-dried packages

He's one of the fittest and most intelligent dads around, but he's also one of the nerdiest, and tends to have a bad haircut. All that helmet-wearing plays havoc with volume.

Even though she's very proud of her high achiever, Space Mom gets annoyed at mealtimes because Space Dad always wants his food in small, freeze-dried packages and is very keen that his food be blended.

The trouble with Space Dad is that whatever you are talking about he will eventually say, "Yes, but up in space things are different." Plus he's dangerous to drive with because he keeps looking up wistfully.

All the same, it feels good to be with him. This dad has an aura and makes you feel like you have perspective.

PART
four

The Family Jigsaw

The Family Jigsaw

No dad is an island. A dad is one part of a network of family relationships, a cobweb of mutual dependency, a diagram of lines and dots that represent people and the connections between them. Dad sometimes has to switch roles—he's certainly a dad, but he might also be a son, a brother, even a husband. So, to understand your dad more deeply, it can help to look at his behavior toward other relations.

Big Brother

Dads often have brothers and sisters. These brothers and sisters are known as aunts and uncles.

Aunts and uncles are there to buy extravagant birthday and Christmas presents for their nephews and nieces. Often they live abroad or are eccentric or undesirable in some way.

"Uncle Bernard let me fly the airplane.... Dad, why aren't you an airline pilot?"

The key thing is that they see your dad not as a dad, but as their brother.

They bring with them all sorts of metaphorical suitcases and skeleton-enriched wardrobes, a whole history of competition and cooperation, struggle and stand-off, hostility and happiness.

Now, many dads get on well with their siblings; their shared histories make them feel grounded and connected.

But not all.

There are some things that can make it difficult for dad to get on with aunts and uncles.

Consider how a dad must feel if he is strapped to a grinding nine-to-five, mortgaged up to his neck, struggling to make various ends meet various other ends, while

Don't worry, bro, I'll cut it just like mine...

his brother, always the family rebel, a sheep of ultimate darkness, a sheep who moved to New York City at the age of sixteen and was the cause of much anxiety and many family squabbles—a sheep who is now on the TV three nights a week in a prime-time sitcom that dad despises with all the emotional powers available to him but which seems to be paying the uncle in question an outrageous amount of money.

Yes, sibling rivalry can certainly affect dads, especially if they are siblings. The trouble with an annoyingly successful brother or sister is that they can outshine a dad in all kinds of unpredictable ways.

Dad may love to see his children happy, but he doesn't really want to hear his son, with uncontained excitement, shrieking, "Dad, Aunt Rosemary took me to the film set and I got to meet Steven Spielberg and he let me do the clapper-board thing and he gave me a baseball cap and he said if I go back next week I can have a walk-on part as an alien!"

Nor does he want to hear, "Dad, Uncle Bernard let me fly the airplane back from Texas! Dad, why aren't you an airline pilot?"

Sometimes it's impossible to compete. It may be best just to accept this.

For while it's tempting to try to even things out, to get some sort of revenge, the trouble is that revenge can often backfire on the revenger.

Hearing something like:

"Dad, I told Uncle Bernard that you said he made the family cat run away by tying it to a fireworks-powered skateboard, and he said that you did that,"

Or,

"Dad, Aunt Rosemary says that lots of women don't get married and you should mind your own business," doesn't improve things.

The kids will just end up angry that their aunts and uncles buy them fewer expensive presents than before. Sometimes dads have no choice but to grit their teeth, smile thinly and say:

"Yes, Uncle Bernard really is a great guy." The reverse of this problem is when an aunt or uncle is less than successful in life (i.e., deeply unsuccessful).

In some ways it's not such a morale-sapping difficulty for dad. Uncle Bernard stumbles from low-paid job to low-paid job, turning up at the house every couple of months, smelling of drink and looking to borrow three hundred dollars for a sure thing at the Belmont Stakes.

Aunt Rosemary becomes harder and harder to understand as she skips merrily into her fifth marriage leaving an ever-widening wake of kids and stepkids behind her.

★ Dad certainly doesn't feel outshone, but he may well feel disappointed, tainted, as well
★ as financially taxed.

★ Dad feels the pull of his original family more strongly if someone else is letting the team down.

tick, tick, tick . . .

"Dad, I told
Uncle Bernard
that you said he
made the family
cat run away
by tying it to a
fireworks-powered
skateboard, and
he said that you
did that"

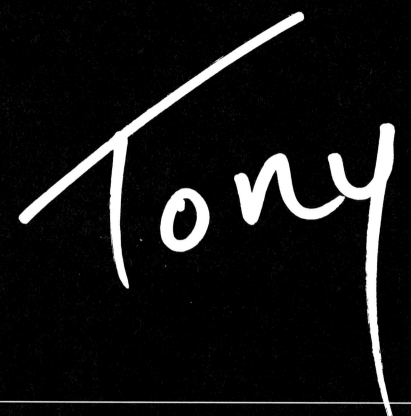

Tony—Mostly spotted in San Francisco and northern California and the Napa wineries. A swarthy, rotund man, flamboyant by nature and most likely sporting some variant of facial hair— be it five-o'clock shadow or for the more mature Tony, a mustache. Tonys like a blazer (single-breasted, double-vented), a belted trouser or big-pocketed chino (on the weekend) and, although ill-advised for the larger man, a penny loafer is Tony's shoe of choice.

In-laws

Even stranger to think about:

Dad has brothers, sisters and parents that aren't his real brothers, sisters and parents (this happens twice if dad was adopted).

They are known as **in-laws.**

Why can't your sister be more like you?

Even the title sounds something like a threat, like a rule that must never be broken, like a series of commitments as strong as steel chains.

The reason that in-law relationships can be difficult, in fact historically are difficult, is that with blood relations there have usually been many years of mutual discovery and symbiotic accommodation; with in-law relationships this is not the case.

Dad has married the love of his life, the one person about whom he never had a single doubt. The same marriage now links him, in law, to another family, a family he probably doesn't know too well, a family he hardly even noticed when he was love-struck and goofy.

In-laws . . . even the title sounds like a threat

His new mother is seemingly kind and friendly toward him, but the relationship has an undercurrent of disappointment, disapproval and, more often than not, disbelief.

His new father is usually totally unable to conceal his suspicion. This suspicion will often reveal itself in hostility, verbal sniping and a general tendency to undermine dad's progress.

Dad's relationships with brothers- and sisters-in-law are unpredictable, ranging from the delightful to the deviant.

The most dangerous outcome of all possible dangerous outcomes is when dad fancies his sister-in-law.

When this happens, the delicate golden threads that link dad to his other family become a nightmarish cobweb that drags all sorts of people toward a sort of central vortex of family-related emotional turmoil.

Without being moralistic in any way, it is fair to say that it is immoral for a dad to act upon his desires for his brother-in-law's keeper.

A dad needs to uphold his status with his own family. To be found by his own child under the sheets with auntie is a fairly good bet as an event that might destroy a child's respect for his or her dad.

In-laws are more than just in-laws.

I will be watching you, I will *always* be watching you....

He's Still My Baby

Let's not forget, dads have dads.

And moms.

They are still sons.

Although they spend much of their time, superficially at least, telling others how it should be, dads themselves still get told what to do too.

Oddly, this is often where they get their wisdom—from experience. Dad does know how it feels; he's been there. He's still there. There is someone whose approval or disapproval still matters.

Dad can still be:

☞ A naughty boy, a fool, a child.

Grandma still says stuff like:

☞ "Don't pick your nose, darling."

And granddad still says stuff like:

☞ "You paid what? Are you deranged?"

Aside from mom, they are the only people who can say stuff like that to dad.

The student of dad, ever in search of paternal enlightenment, is interested in how ★ dad reacts to grandma and granddad.

★ Like father like son. Monkey see; monkey do. All that.
★

Is dad confident in his status as dad, or does he slide back into an infantile state, which always annoys mom to the point where she chews her hair and calls dad by his actual name?

Becoming a dad should, perhaps and possibly, be a significant point of release, a letting-go, not only adopting a new role but shedding an old one.

But that's all easily said. If dad still shows his bank statements and bills to his dad, he may not have cut the eminently cuttable ties that bind. The same goes for passing on to mom the domestic commentary of his mom—observations about tidiness, femininity, maternal qualities.

Mister Lover Man

Before dad gets to be a dad, he is a lover.

It can be that dad is a lover only once, but most dads slide into domesticity all too quickly. They get married or live in sin.

So it's likely that dad has had a previous life, a pre-dad persona, a romancing-mom persona. This kind of thing is notoriously difficult for offspring to think about.

Parents are parents: bland characters who ask about school and tell you when you can leave the table. They are not hot-blooded, bed-sheet-ruffling, animalistic cavorters.

Oh, but they are. Or they certainly were, and, knowing dad, something is still going on.

PART
FIVE

G

The Gospel
According to Dad

Blah, blah . . .

The Gospel According to Dad

The experienced dad has much to teach the newcomer. All that experience, for one thing. The terrors and the tears, from infancy to adulthood. Those badges of honor—chicken pox, swimming clubs, broken limbs, PTA meetings. When children go through phases, so do parents—phases of reaction to their children's phases—and they pay an emotional price. The price, however, can be reduced. Knowing how to be a good dad requires a complex toolkit. Fear not, though. That knowledge can be communicated in writing. Here, bringing all the bacon back home, dad tells it like it is.

The Credo

I am a dad. It's how I see myself; it's who I am. I live it; I breathe it; I love it. And I pride myself on how seriously I take my role. If someone comes up to me in the street and asks me what it's all about, I've got absolutely no doubt about my answer—it's all about the kids. That's what it's all about. The kids. My kids. And I dedicate myself to bringing them up right.

Amen

Walking & Talking

Kids become more interesting when they get properly mobile and start chattering.

But once they start shuffling and staggering about and asking all sorts of ridiculous questions, your life gets even busier.

What should you do with these babbling bundles of fun?

The answer: you have to interact with them.

Keep a close eye on the kids when they're learning to walk because they like to launch themselves, face-first, toward just about any type of pointed sharp thing.

You have to watch the toddler for as long as they do that Frankenstein's monster walk. Let them hold your hand when they are getting started.

Or, if you don't like vacating the armchair every five minutes, set up a series of cables at about eighteen inches above the floor, so the little tykes have something to hold on to in the early upright stages.

The main thing about children and speech development is swearing.

You have to retrain yourself first of all. A good method is to imagine that your grandma is always with you.

You probably won't want to do too much cussing in front of her, so you won't do it in front of the youngsters.

You really do have to try to cut it out, because they will pick it up before you can say "********ing m*********er."

I always think there's nothing worse than a two-year-old yapping profanities at security guards in a shopping center.

Always remember to stop imagining that grandma is with you when the babbler goes to bed.

If you don't, things get sort of odd.

grandma

Meals

At Home

Even once the patter of tiny feet is well and truly familiar, and the breast and the bottle are gone (for the kid), mealtimes probably won't get back to what they once were.

It's amazing how long it takes children to learn how to use cutlery successfully. They're dreadful.

Even during the teenage years they are not averse to the occasional catapulted fork, or tantrum-induced drink spillage.

Breakfast becomes a hectic scramble of getting the little people schoolworthy and fed.

Although you might want them to eat oatmeal or a little lightly buttered toast with organic orange marmalade, they will want the most expensive, sugar-encrusted, children's-TV-promotional-molded-plastic-"toy"-giveaway-sponsored cereal available.

Unless you are a dad of superhuman abilities, or mom disciplines the kids, you will give it to them.

Other meals are a struggle of wills.

Once fully into solid foods, junior humans begin to get picky about what they will and won't eat. And when they get picky, meals get tricky.

Mrs. Dad has spent hours in the kitchen preparing lots of home-cooked, nutritious grub for the wee ones, and she gets all depressed when they clamp their lips

and turn their heads and start screeching about how they want SpaghettiOs or fish sticks. And when she gets depressed . . . dads need some strategies when it comes to getting vegetables into the kids.

Simply mixing it in won't always do it. Some people use food coloring to con their toddlers into eating "greens."

> Some people use food coloring to con their toddlers into eating "greens." It's a bit dishonest, though. I prefer straight bribery

It's a bit dishonest, though. I prefer straight bribery.

In my experience, children respond very well to money from an early age. It has to be small amounts and there has to be a cut-off point.

Another option is "parcel" food: spinach in ravioli, that type of thing. Be prepared for food difficulties up until the apples of your eyes finally fly their free-range nest.

Eating Out

A risky venture. Even the most strictly brought-up children are liable to run amok in a restaurant.

The food will be different to food at home, and, in terms of their environment, there are too many possibilities open to them.

Food-laden waiters, carts of steaming victuals and wildly swinging kitchen doors are like magnets to the under-fives.

People tend to be reasonably forgiving when you take toddlers to restaurants. As they get older, the problem becomes more about sullen or rude behavior.

Appealing to their better judgment is always worth a try with young teenagers.

Sometimes, though, you just have to put them in their place—tell the waitress that:

"He's depressed because school has kept him back a year for the third time,"

Or,

"She's feeling nauseous because she just found out where babies come from."

Give us a break, they aren't fish sticks!

Behavior

It isn't long before your beautiful gurgling babies, newly liberated by the skills of walking and talking, are turning into rage-fueled, self-obsessed, violent psychopaths.

In between short periods of smiling and falling asleep, bleary-eyed, on your shoulder, they begin to snatch and bite and gouge and hit and scream and throw themselves around. All the kinds of behavior you might expect from totally egocentric beings.

Your job is to turn these wild animals into caring, thoughtful, social creatures. Not surprisingly, it's a bit of a life's-work scenario.

Lying is actually funny initially. They do it so badly.

When you find your child with paint all over her face and clothes, sitting next to a three-

> You have to tell them more than once that punching little Michael and stealing his toys is not a nice thing to do

foot-high signed self-portrait on the wall next to her bed and she claims to have no knowledge of how it got there, it's hard not to laugh.

As they get older and their lying becomes increasingly sophisticated, you sometimes admire their imagination.

It is possible, with hard work and patience, to foster an environment of complete honesty and openness, an atmosphere in which your children will want to share and communicate their thoughts and feelings. It can be done.

But, as I say, it's hard work and I could never see why my kids shouldn't live in self-serving denial like everybody else.

In many families the behavior of siblings toward each other is the biggest headache.

★ All the He started it/No she started it stuff can be pretty tiresome. You have to tell them
★ more than once that punching little Norman and stealing his toys is not a nice thing to do.
★

You have to tell them this repeatedly for a number of years before it finally gets through.

The danger here, and it's not infrequent, is that the siblings really will fall out and become distant and unfriendly in adulthood.

There isn't necessarily that much that you can do. They are who they are. The best you can do is to try to keep the family together while they are still at home.

If they are still friends at eighteen they stand a good chance. Once they go, however, as with all things, it's up to them.

Pets

Pets become desirable to children from about the age of five.

Pets bring out the best and the worst in them:

The best in that they want to love and care for something.

The worst in that they want to love and care for something without actually making the effort to clean, feed, water, exercise, etc.

Although letting your children keep pets can be a chore, it's an effective way of teaching them a number of life's lessons. Chores and responsibility, for starters.

And pets teach kids other important facts too, facts about procreation and death in particular.

They act as prompts for Q&A sessions. So be ready suddenly to hear:

"Daddy, Princess and Boomer are playing piggyback!"

Or,

"Lucky's fallen asleep and gone all stiff!"

You can use these spontaneous conversations to inform the kids about the birds and the bees without involving mommy and daddy and the attendant unpleasant imagery this brings.

Be in no doubt, you need delicacy and subtlety in order to get it right. You will have to judge what sort of information can be managed by the emotional maturity of your child.

"That's just the way guinea pigs hug when they love each other," might be enough for one child.

Another might need to know that, "Well, Catherine is in estrus and Cuthbert can sense this, is aroused and so attempts to mate with her. The growling is just a noise daddies, I mean guinea pigs, make when they're happy in a particular way."

So, pets can be good things for the development of your whippersnapper, but it does all depend on the age of the kids and your own home circumstances.

> **A dad is *not* just for Christmas. . . .**

It may be fashionable for those living in urban areas to keep a pit bull in the bathroom or an Asian python in the closet, but my advice is not to go leaping into anything drastic.

Start small.

Hamsters and mice don't take too much looking after and do introduce little ones to the painful fact that something small, cute and fluffy can bite your fingernail off if you are not careful.

A couple of tiny rodents in a cage should allow you to gauge whether or not little Emily is ready for the responsibility.

If she's not, they don't live too long.

Rabbits and guinea pigs are the next step up. They take a bit more looking after (they live longer too) and draw a bit more blood when they bite.

Of course cats and dogs are top of the list as they interact in a meaningful way with people, and this is what all the years of children's fiction have taught kids to expect from anything with fur.

Cats don't take too much looking after, but all the interaction has to be on their terms.

Dogs have that loyalty and enthusiasm thing going for them, but they need walking a lot, and that will fall to you, because most kids cannot commit to anything other than themselves for the kind of period of time a dog might be expected to live.

That's just the way guinea pigs hug when they love each other

Bicycles

What is a bicycle?

A bicycle is not just an economical means of short-distance transportation. A bicycle is a beautiful piece of precision engineering that can inspire the imaginations of young minds; a bicycle is a possession that can give a sense of freedom, adventure, skill and responsibility to its young owner; a bicycle is a totemic object, allowing dads to bond with their kids while taking part in an informal but memorable and important rite of passage. Even those little girls' bikes that are pink and have streamers coming off the handlebars.

And what is there to know?

Oiling gears, replacing brake blocks and fixing punctures is easy stuff. The bicycle— with all its technological complexities and the mystical skills of its operation—is a great thing for dad to be an expert about.

And forget not that the bicycle allows dads to take part in the generational ritual of learnin' the young 'uns to ride. You'll get one of those delightful flashbacks that you start getting when you've got kids, remembering your own dad walking along behind you, one hand gripping the seat, the other an open copy of *Hot Rod Enthusiast*.

It's best to teach your kids to learn to ride on grass rather than tarmac or gravel. Over-enthusiastic dads can go down too.

Bikes are also a good way of keeping kids fit and active rather than slumped comatose in front of some unbelievably violent video game.

And family bike rides are as good a way as any of giving your kids the opportunity to bicker, sulk, injure or kill themselves while getting a little exercise.

You do, as with all things, need to be especially careful where teenage boys are concerned. They like to ride them off roofs or through nursing homes and so on.

Be prepared to confiscate a bike in times of crisis.

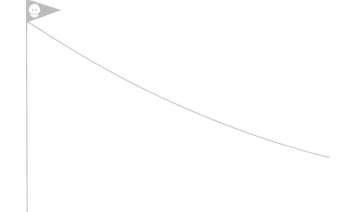

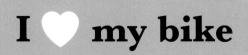

I ♥ my bike

Ray—A close, yet poorer relation of Tony. He sells books, but would give it all up tomorrow to go back to selling cars. Due to a thirty-year diet of Budweiser and fried foods, Ray is impotent. Never out of his one suit, even on the beach, as far as Ray is concerned fashion is the preserve of "queers and lebanons."

Vacations

If you're looking for the highs and lows of a dad's life, look no further than the family vacation.

Those two weeks in the summer are a fantastic opportunity to enjoy new and exciting experiences as a family, to have fun, to share time together.

An opportunity from which there is no escape.

Planes, trains, buses and cars, airports, ferry terminals, Roman amphitheaters—Dad has to keep it all together.

In some ways this is good, you are exercising your dad power. But you need to be on the ball, as there are so many unpredictable variables. Not least, your own kids.

In the Car

Long car rides, of the sort that punctuate many trips, are notoriously boring for children.

It's okay for dad, at least he's got a seemingly endless and uniform highway to focus on, and Mrs. Dad can spend the trip imagining how she's going to spend dad's money when they get there.

But the kids . . . it's not fair to expect them to count how many red cars there are for up to four and a half hours.

There is no easy solution. Modern technology seems to offer, as ever at a price, a means of unlimited entertainment for the kids while on car journeys:

The headrest DVD player. An easy solution!

Again, modernity is encouraging our offspring to be passive, unthinking blobs, which isn't the end of the world for half a day's road trip, but it is somehow dispiriting and there ought to be a better way.

And, do you really want to be doing seventy in the fast lane, overtaking a poorly loaded articulated truck in a cloud of visibility-reducing spray, while listening to uncontrolled wailing from the backseat because Bambi's mother has just been killed?

Surely I-Spy is better, not to mention a whole lot cheaper, than that.

It's obviously not true to say that whether you opt for Boston or Brazil the dad experience is the same. But there will be similarities.

You are the leader, so expect the wife and kids to look to you for leadership.

I spy, with my little eye, something beginning with D . . .

A lot of this leadership is of a financial kind. Dad pays for the pony ride just as he does for the half day of white-water rafting.

But it isn't all to do with digging your wallet out and doing a quick mini-statement in your head. Your leadership must be physical, psychological and moral too.

That means that when things are looking grim and the voice in your head is saying, "You are lost in a Guatemalan rain forest," you need to be able to smile and put on that confident wink when you tell them everything's going to be fine.

Traveling itself, the sitting in a vehicle of some kind or lining up for a ticket or waiting in an airport, can be grueling enough for the grown-ups.

For the coiled springs of energy that are children it is the equivalent of enforced captivity.

In this kind of scenario, upbringing comes into its own. Ask yourself—you're in the airport, baggage all checked, waiting for an announcement.

When it comes it smacks you with a three-hour delay. You look to your children. They shrug and smile at you and turn back to their Dickens and Austen respectively.

Or, the brats run off screaming at the announcement, only to reappear some forty minutes later, when, through the great glass window that overlooks the airplanes, you notice not only armed police on the tarmac but above them your offspring jumping up and down on the wing of a refueling Boeing.

★ Which do you want? That's the difference upbringing can make in an airport
★ catastrophe situation.

★ Airports, ferries and foreignness of any kind can be easily avoided by vacationing at home.

Not "at home" in that you set up a tent in your own garden (though, if you start early enough, most kids will accept this as going on vacation), but "at home" in that you don't leave the country.

Why would you want to go abroad? After all, it's not as if the countryside at home is ruined by road building, new housing and out-of-town shopping; and it's not as if the beaches here are crowded and polluted and commercialized almost to the point of being declared disaster areas by FEMA.

In fact, thinking about it, if you really want to ensure that your children do not take their lives for granted, two weeks in a coastal vacation camp will probably be enough.

Abroad

Once upon a time, this word, for me at least, conjured images of long, white, empty beaches reflecting dazzlingly bright sunlight and lapped by azure waves, sipping iced cocktails under a banana leaf parasol and thinking how good Mrs. Dad looks in her new bikini.

I can still just about remember those days, long gone though they may be.

It's the sort of stuff to keep your memory warm through the long dark months of winter (which isn't, but could be, a metaphor for the years of raising kids).

Anyway, once little ones turn up, going abroad does lose its romance slightly. Having said that, abroad is a great place to take your kids.

Abroad, if you avoid all the right places, can be so different and so inspiring for the curiosity of young minds:

"Daddy, why don't we live in a mud hut?"

"Daddy, doesn't that snake by your foot look like the one in the guidebook?"

That type of thing.

It is, of course, a cliché, and thus both true and untrue, that travel broadens the mind.

Youngsters should be having their minds broadened by school and books and growing up in general.

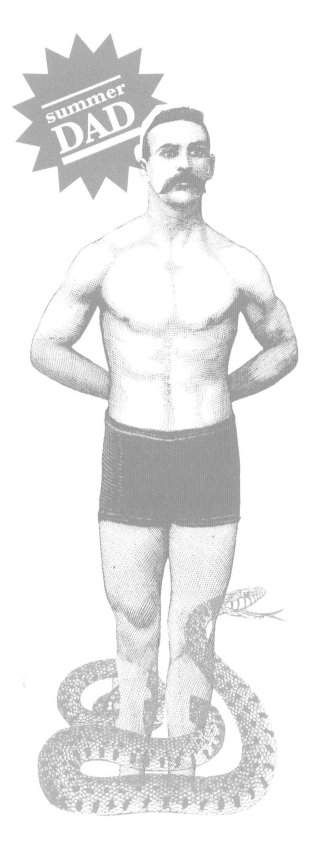

summer
DAD

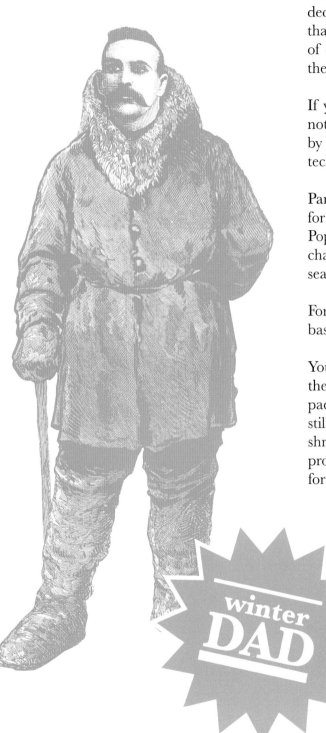

But foreign travel and its attendant lack of decent TV programs should teach your kids that there are those, particularly in the area of children's TV, much less fortunate than they are.

If you are worried that your children might not adapt well to going abroad, start off by visiting one of those destinations that is technically abroad but doesn't feel like it.

Parts of Mexico and the Caribbean are good for this (Barbados, Antigua, St. Lucia, etc.). Popular choices all, because they are not too challenging for the family that wants sun, sea, sand and hamburgers and french fries.

For dad the advantages are familiar beer and baseball on satellite.

Your children will be able to bask in the sun as they build sandcastles and paddle in the ever-calm shallows, yet still be able to hear, and understand, the shrill scream of a margaritaed mom yelling profane abuse at her four-year-old for "nickin' my cigs."

winter DAD

Daddy, doesn't that snake by your feet look like the one from the guidebook?

Birthdays & So On

Obviously the first thing that needs to be said about the children's birthdays is that they must never be forgotten.

Forgetting your child's birthday is one of the main signs of being a bad dad.

Thankfully, Mrs. Dad will probably remind you that a birthday is coming up and you can mumble in a "don't patronize me" tone about how you knew the birthday was coming up anyway, you just hadn't gotten around to buying a present and a card.

Birthdays serve a number of functions:

First, they remind you how old your children are, how close they are to school age or driving lessons or criminal responsibility.

Second, they are an excuse, like anyone needs one, to spoil your kids with gifts that they won't appreciate or that reflect your interests rather than theirs.

Third, they set you off on the road of children's parties—balloons and clowns and magicians that make you think that your mediocre and frustrating life really isn't so bad after all.

What you will discover is that these parties, ostensibly for the benefit of sugar-addled young ones, are in fact yet another way for competitive parents to square up to one another.

It wouldn't be so bad if you could just shrug your shoulders and have nothing to do with it. But that's not possible.

If you want your kids to keep being invited, which you probably do, then you have to do your bit, knuckle down and phone that alcoholic balloon guy.

And you have to make sure that all the "guests" leave with a goody bag that's better than the last one they got.

It sometimes seems that all this is going to end with dads taking out second mortgages so young Jessica's "guests" can all go home with their very own Arabian racehorse.

Mrs. Dad's Day

As well as remembering birthdays, there is one other date it is your duty to remember:

Mother's Day.

They make it difficult by moving the date, but it's two or three weeks before Memorial Day.

Mother's Day is a good opportunity to spoil Mrs. Dad—do it well and you get points for days—and she likes it when the kids are involved. They love making cards and going along with the whole "No, you put your feet up" thing.

You don't have to worry about Father's Day. When it comes, make it yours.

I'm so sorry, it's just too much to remember. . . .

Christmas

How do you remember Christmas?

A magical time of presents and chocolates and a huge and excessive roast turkey lunch?

A steady buildup of expectation and excitement with tree decorating and advent calendars marking the days left before the great event?

Did you leave out apple pies, a couple of large scotches and ten Marlboro Reds for Santa?

And then, gradually, the shine was lost, the glittery magic revealed itself to be mass-produced and tawdry, the stories about Santa and the reindeer were just stories, and the celebration of Christ's birth started to seem like an odd, questionable, exploited anachronism.

Well, guess what? When kids arrive the whole thing gets going again. The presents, the decorations, the fun, the family dinner— it all comes flooding back. Years of it.

It's easier and more fun just to go along with the thing and enjoy watching them unwrap their ★ ponies and their ★ robot dinosaurs

★

You can tell your children all about the winter equinox and pagan religion and Saturnalia and Emperor Constantine, but that conversation can surely wait.

While they're still young enough to believe, it's easier and more fun just to go along with the thing and enjoy watching them unwrap their ponies and their robot dinosaurs.

If you still live where nativity plays are held, don't miss them. They are hilarious and heart-warming, and usually give you a couple of classic lines that bear repeating—"My brother's a sheep," "Jesus is crying," stuff like that.

School

In some ways I always wanted to homeschool my brood. But you need to be really clever and fairly well off to do it, so it never really worked out.

It would have been a mistake anyway. Because you never can tell. I didn't get on with school at all.

My kids loved it. Where's the logic?

Whether your young 'uns love school or hate it, or both, there are phases. These phases

are elementary, middle and high schools. The most important thing is to make sure they are going to the right ones at the right time.

You may still remember your first day at school. Lots of people do.

It's a time of great seriousness and anxiety on the part of many children. In a way that is new to them they are being made to take one of those large early strides we all take toward being a big boy or girl.

They are realizing that they will grow up, are growing up, and they want it and are afraid of it.

There is only so much a dad can do. You have to sympathize yet you have to impart resolve and enthusiasm as well. It can be hard when they're all tearful and saying they've been to school enough and their heads are full and why do they need to go again.

You have to stick with it and wait for the day when the *What did you do today?* question is greeted with a babbling cascade of excitement.

> In my day you wanted shoes that left a special footprint behind. . . . Now you have to have sneakers with a built-in camera and Internet access

The step to middle school is often a difficult one. From being the big fish in a little pool, they suddenly become the littlest fish in a great big institutional ocean of large aquatic mammals.

Oh my God, Billy! Isn't that your mom?

They feel vulnerable and they are.

Educational expectations increase too. More exams, more people droning on at them about how important the exams are to their prospects in life.

Middle school is also the right sort of place to meet the wrong sort. You have to keep more of an eye on your kids' associates. Try to impress upon them the fact that they do not want a criminal record when applying for jobs.

Uniform isn't a problem until the middle school years, when teenagers get all image conscious and insist on a particular pair of pants or a certain pair of shoes. This is a phase that they will grow out of, or, if they don't, once they leave home you no longer have to pay for it.

The trouble is that the special jeans or the trendy footwear are usually the most expensive versions available.

Perhaps it's all relative: in my day you wanted shoes that left a special footprint behind—animal tracks or some sort of code. Now you have to have sneakers with a built-in camera and Internet access.

Another thing about middle schools is that they seem to be becoming places where the student ethos is about being "cool" rather than actually learning anything. In fact the two ideas are believed to be mutually exclusive.

★ Obviously, as a dad, you have to work against this. Your goal might end up being
★ to convince your children that education is a valuable and desirable thing. Part of
★ your problem is that you're probably not deemed "cool" yourself, so finding a way to be persuasive is a tough nut to crack.

I have not always seen eye to eye with Mrs. Dad about this. My initial plan—to trounce the kids weekly at Trivial Pursuit—resulted in the junior members of the household becoming moody and retreating to their bedrooms whenever I got the box out.

My second plan—to make them work on a building site for a year before letting them study for the SATs—was rejected outright by the missus.

I still say it could have worked. Yes, they're doing okay, but who knows what might have been?

Extracurricular

Your growing youths will be keen to try new things.

They will suffer crazes and enthusiasms. They will want stuff.

As a dad, you want for your children all the opportunities you never had and all that. It might be piano or dance lessons (the latter perhaps not being something about which you have huge regrets), or to join the football team or get a skateboard or learn to ride llamas or those tiny little motorbikes.

Much of what you are able to give your children in terms of opportunities and skills depends on how much money you have.

Not everyone can afford to buy a pony and a paddock.

Sport

Sports are clearly a good way for your kids to keep fit and healthy.

And most sports don't cost that much— the price of a pair of baseball cleats might seem a bit steep when you're in the shop shelling out the cash, but it's usually a good investment.

If your seven-year-old tells you he wants to take up polo, however, your contributions for the same amount of fitness and teamwork are going to be steeper still.

Look on the bright side: he might marry into serious money. It's not necessarily about class anyway—a croquet set isn't all that expensive.

Music

In the case of children learning music, it is often, though not always, about whether they come from a "musical family."

Schools can help with music lessons, access to instruments, and so on. So get the kids to try playing a clarinet at school before reaching for your wallet.

They sometimes find that it's harder than it looks or that practicing is boring. If they do seem intent on following a musical path, try to steer them away from costly instruments like grand pianos. Drums aren't good either—you'll be listening to whatever it is for years to come.

"People try to put us d-d-d-down . . ."

Screeeeeeeeeeetccchhhhhh!!!

The Talk

Obviously the talk is a father-and-son thing.
It's another rite of passage.

"Son, how much do you know about
women?"

I never did it, or gave it. They get enough of
it at school—Johnny Has Three Grandmas
or whatever it's called—what can I tell them?

I felt I had to try, so I asked my eldest, he
must have been twelve, if he knew about sex.
He said he did, so I left it at that. I found
myself falling back on the old Dad bottom
line: I survived without it.

**Gary, I need to
talk to you about
the miracle
of life. . . .**

**What would you
like to know, Dad?**

Girlfriends & Boyfriends

When your kids start getting crushes and falling in love, you can't help having a viewpoint.

It's also when all your sexist assumptions will rise up like colored smoke to obscure this view.

The way dad reacts to his son having a girlfriend is not exactly the same as the way he reacts when a daughter is involved with a boy.

If you react emotionally instead of rationally, a daughter can end up feeling that she is not allowed the same kind of freedom as her brother when it comes to going out and socializing. But acting rationally is not easy at this point.

If you think about it, your attitude to a son's romantic escapades is bound to be indulgent—he's like you.

On the other hand, a daughter is someone who needs your protection, who is fragile and naive and who doesn't realize that the debonair but heartless misogynist is a common character in life's narrative.

It's best just to leave dealing with your daughter's love life to Mrs. Dad. She is pretty shrewd about all this. After all, she makes good choices.

That's my boy!

PART

SIX

P
The Psychology of Dad

The Psychology of Dad

Hold on to your hat, here comes the psychology. The study of dad is full of enlightening stuff with which to enlighten us. Theories, complexes, repressions, sublimations—who'd have thought being a dad was so complicated, so fraught? Well, in one sense it isn't. That's right. The great thing about psychology is that you don't have to know anything. Or even do anything. Just do what comes "naturally" and you're there.

Pop Psychology

It probably means something about not looking at your tennis opponent when shaking hands. Or a vague awareness that some people say you have an inner child and turn into the parent you least expected.

If you are of a sensitive, imaginative disposition, you may wish to look away now

Safe to say that the dad on the street doesn't know much.

It's time to make room on your plate for penis envy, castration anxiety, Electra and Oedipus complexes, your id, your ego and your superego. An awesome smorgasbord if ever there was one.

And in terms that mix the metaphors of consumption with those of perspective, psychology gives you a weird, otherworldly kaleidoscope to chew on while thinking about dadness.

But it is scary and unpleasant, so, if you are of a sensitive, imaginative disposition, you may wish to look away now.

Parental Advisory

So what, you ask, is penis envy, and how does it affect being a dad?

According to Freudian theory, girls, as part of their psycho-sexual development (steady your nerves, dear reader, worse is to come. Much worse), realize that they do not have a penis. This realization causes them to envy and to want their father's penis.

(If you are feeling queasy at this point, dear dad, take a couple of breaths.)

Quite why they should feel not having a penis is a thing to be regretted is unexplained. The best thing for dads to do is pretend none of this exists. In all likelihood it will go away and need never be spoken of. Hooray for that.

And the same goes for castration anxiety. If you are worried about it, again, doing nothing—a true dad solution—will probably work. After all, telling your young son, as some kind of reassuring boost, that he has great-looking genitals is not really going to help your father-son relationship in the long run.

Freud reckons dad is the power in the family because he has the best and the original penis, and that all the kids envy it. One way around this is to make sure your kids never see you naked. Let them live their lives in the assumption that you have no reproductive organs at all. This is not as easy as it sounds, but can be achieved with the help of swimming trunks and occasionally just telling the youngsters to face the wall.

Psychology is more interesting when considering dad's role in the development of his kids' personalities, values, ambitions and all that. It got pretty fashionable in the late twentieth century to lament the family, to portray that most universal of units as a bear pit of lunacy and neuroses.

Everyone lined up to point an accusing finger at mom and dad as the source of all weakness and woe. This is not to say that your parents might not, you know, f*** you up. But it's not guaranteed. Some good, solid dad action can work wonders when it comes to producing rounded and sane offspring.

Dad is the power in the family because he has the best and the original penis

What being the possessor of the family's best penis really means is that dad has to set the standard for masculinity. Whatever that means.

After all, it's a postfeminist world. Whatever that means.

Whether you're living in the first or twenty-first century, the qualities of masculinity are inextricably linked to the qualities of dad. Becoming a dad is a sign of potency, which is at the heart of the essence of the kernel of what being male means. Whatever that means.

It's not a skirt, it's a Japanese Night Fighting Suit!

I'm a Matcho, Matcho Man!

Role Muddle

Masculine values, if you believe in such things, are, obviously, best passed on to boys. Mom can be relied on to show daughters how to apply makeup, use credit cards, collect jewelry, smoke a tampon, etc.

But, make no mistake about it—dad is a valuable model for daughters:

Dad teaches them something about the solidity of males:

☞ Dads sit there and listen to you cry, and talk slowly and reassuringly in their low voices.

☞ Dads come out in the car.

☞ Dads get out the checkbook.

Daughters are more forgiving of dad and his dad ways than mom is. Mom knows what dad once was and can see only the terrible dereliction that has befallen him. His daughter sees only dad.

He's only ever worn a vest and shorts; he's only ever been 200 pounds. As far as she's concerned, all dads spend entire weekends in the attic building a reconstruction of Apollo 11 from matchsticks.

And, ironically and rather gloomily, dad's failures will prepare her, psychologically speaking that is, for inadequacies in her own marriage. Thus the circle of life completes.

Er, Luton, we have a problem

Robin—Usually married to Fiona and most often found with three teenage kids (Zak, Solomon and Daisy), Robin is fervently antinuclear, an avid recycler, and enjoys the excellent driving position of his brand-new S-Class Mercedes. An architect by trade, and stupendously rich, Robin has always struggled with the private/state school dilemma.

PART
SEVEN

The Natural Dad

The Natural Dad

Psychology is all well and good. But psychological inquiry raises the study of dad to an otherworldly level of great complexity. For many people this can cause headaches and temporary blindness. There are other ways of studying the paternal existence. A nice, straightforward method of inquiry is to look at the way that other members of the animal kingdom, animal dads, that is, go about their everyday fatherly business.

Miniature Masculinity

The phrase "Alpha Male" tends to conjure images of massive gorillas towering upright on their legs, beating their beautiful silvery chests and baring powerful and sharp-looking teeth in an attempt to intimidate other males into accepting that none of those dishy female gorillas over there are currently available.

If, however, there were an "Alpha Dad," it probably wouldn't be a gorilla. It might be, of all things, the lowly sea horse—*Hippocampus* himself.

The sea horse is not famous for uncontained and savage aggression, even though it does sometimes get involved in what you might describe as small-scale underwater head-butting contests.

It is famous for a particularly unusual quality in the world of masculinity and particularly in the world of fatherhood. Mr. Sea Horse, all three centimeters of him, is one of Nature's supreme dads.

The understanding, thoroughly decent Mr. Sea Horse is prepared to let Mrs. Sea Horse do the penetrating. Youch, what a guy

Not for him a determination, once pregnancy and imminent fatherhood are confirmed, to continue the life of the pre-dad male—down the boozer, out with his buddies, flirting with the unattached mares.

No. Mr. Sea Horse is the one that gets pregnant. And not only that. The understanding, thoroughly decent Mr. Sea Horse is prepared to let Mrs. Sea Horse do the penetrating. Youch, what a guy.

Then, to top it all off, in something like the life of a miniature subaqua kangaroo, he carries the fertilized eggs around in his pouch for several weeks. Mr. Sea Horse is the one to experience the miracle of birth.

Respect that dad! Or pity him! Your call.

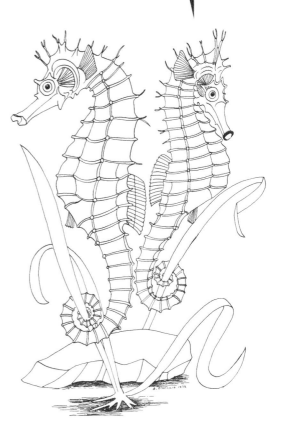

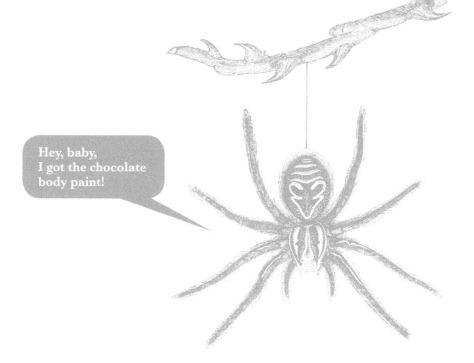

Sex Machine

In terms of sacrifice for the cause, however, Mr. Sea Horse's preparedness to carry the eggs for a couple of weeks is nothing compared to what Mr. Redback Spider is ready to undertake.

In fact, he's not even doing it for his kids; he's doing it for his sperm. That is the very essence of fatherly pride

In most species of spider the male is considerably smaller than the female and mating can be a dangerous pursuit, particularly if the female gets postcoitally peckish. The majority of male spiders have to leg it as soon as the arachnid loving is over.

Not so the redback. The selfless Mr. Redback brings new meaning to the phrase "death wish." Redback Dad—half the size of his paramour—isn't afraid of being snacked up after delivering his gift.

Indeed he goes out of his way to encourage his partner to eat him. During the mating process he positions himself to make it easier for Mrs. Redback to chomp away at his abdomen while he, still smiling enigmatically, continues to make his contribution with the parts of his body that remain. Beat that, foot fetishists.

Here is a dad who should inspire admiration in us all. He is prepared to sacrifice himself for his kids—kids he will never even meet.

In fact, he's not even doing it for his kids; he's doing it for his sperm. That is the very essence of fatherly pride.

And, while the whole thing may strike the average human reader like some nightmarish vision from the film *Alien*, dads will understand the redback's sacrifice as one end of a spectrum of behaviors that can be grouped under the heading—*Kids Come First*.

It does have to be said that the redback consequently misses out on lots of dad stuff, like teaching the young ones to ride a bike or play table tennis or inject venom successfully so that your food is always fresh because it's actually still alive.

This is where the magic happens!

Yo, Dad, turn the heating down!

Dad Endures

For dad stamina no one can compete with the emperor penguin.

But Emperor Penguin Dad has no choice. In true dad style, he just gets on with it

After mating season, female emperor penguins produce a single egg. Once they've done this, they pass the egg to Emperor Penguin Dad, who has to look after it and keep it, and himself, alive through the Antarctic winter, while Emperor Penguin Mom goes back to sea for several months to fill up on fish and squid and hang out with the girls. The nerve.

While child care for human dads usually means dropping the youngster off somewhere on the way to work, all the Emperor Penguin Dads huddle together in the bleak and freezing wilderness and play their parts in forming a giant snowy crèche.

The slowly rotating crèche is a great example of the power of dads in Nature. While this can't be described as a "hands-on" kind of fatherhood—the penguins have no hands—it certainly requires a level of commitment that many human Dads would balk at.

But Emperor Penguin Dad has no choice. In true dad style, he just gets on with it. He keeps his egg warm in a brood pouch, which doesn't sound very dadlike, but nevertheless is a serious macho business in the worldview of the penguin. More macho, say, than a man bag.

Gary

Gary—The youngest child of three, a suspicious seven years after number two, Gary has found solace in a wardrobe full of matching tracksuits and his better-than-average soccer skills.

His Majesty

Mirror mirror, etc.—who is the machoest natural dad of all?

What you really want if you are a wild animal dad is not just to be seen as the patriarch of your family. What you want is to be acknowledged as the supreme something, the pinnacle of a whole environment.

Cue the king of the jungle: Lion Dad.

The male lion even has a special hairdo to make him stand out and seem more regal. His mane is an indicator of his virility—big mane equals much macho potency and potential.

That may be comparable to human appearance and explain why bald men are seen as less sexually desirable. However, these hairless wonders make up for it by being high-earning investment bankers, accountants, Soviet leaders and suchlike—employing optional mate-attracting strategy not available to lions.

Not only does lordly Leo slack off most of the time, he leaves the gazelle, wildebeest and antelope hunting to Mrs. Lion

There are more connections to be made. For 80 percent of the day Lion Dad does nothing, preferring to lounge around and sleep in the shade. Sound familiar?

Not only does lordly Leo slack off most of the time, he leaves the gazelle, wildebeest and antelope hunting to Mrs. Lion, just like Mrs. Dad hunting for 2-for-1s, Club Card points earners and home-brand products in Price Chopper during the weekly grocery shopping.

But, Lion Dad, regal and awesome though he is, is still as much a victim of merciless Nature as he is an example of it. His opportunity for leading and being able to defend his own pride is brief, probably a couple of years at the most.

The pressure on the king of the jungle can lead to some truly shocking behavior. When a male takes over a pride, he will need to kill any cubs fathered by his predecessor, in order that the new Mrs. Lions become receptive to his charms. It's simple and it's brutal. And it is in no way like the dads that we know or may be.

Killing stepchildren is wrong. The lion, remember, is king of the jungle. And people have spent centuries trying to civilize the jungle out of human life. He's handsome, he's powerful, he's emblematic: but he's not like us.

I'm going down to Price Chopper. I'll be back shortly.

If there's any justice in the world . . .

The King of the Swingers

The Darwinian take on evolution would suggest that the paternal practices of gorillas, orangutans and chimpanzees can shed some light on the unlit parts of dad. Knowing where you've come from to know where you're going, etc.

Surely the great apes, with their knowing expressions, apparent laughter and complex social lives, are more instructive when we think of our own behavior and motivation.

Well, you might think that. But, you know, Nature doesn't adhere to Disney's rules. Sure, chimps can ride bicycles and smoke cigarettes, but, according to films and so on, they can wield clubs and grimace menacingly too. So, don't expect it to be all good news from the front lines of simian similarity simulation.

As every schoolboy knows, primates range from humans—at the top needless to say—all the way down to lemurs. So what does Lemur Dad have to tell us about the Art of Dad in general? Well, surprise surprise, Lemur Dad lives under the thumb.

Lemurs live in small social groups where the top lemur is a female. So he has an immediate connection with his Homo sapiens cousins there. Ouch.

Like all primates, Lemur Dad needs to work his way up if he is to become the dominant dad. And he has to compete for Lemur Mom. The competition for Lemur Mom involves rubbing your scent on your tail and waving it about in front of her face: the primate equivalent of wearing a Ralph Lauren shirt and Hugo Boss aftershave—just as offensive and just as likely to work.

Gorilla Dad

People are not lemurs. That much seems clear. Then perhaps they are more like gorillas. Gorillas have had a century of bad press thanks to King Kong and all that. We know now that gorillas are not the monstrous, skyscraper-climbing nutters we once thought. They are mild-mannered vegetarians and highly tolerant of documentary filmmakers.

This great power gives him ultimate responsibility

In fact, Gorilla Dad is, it turns out, one of Nature's top dads. The reason? It's his combination of awesome power and gentleness toward the young that make him such a great example.

Just like Human Dad (in some cases) he has the most physical power and experience in the troop. This great power gives him ultimate responsibility. If there are problems—the gorilla equivalent of a cracked water pipe, a leaky faucet, a flat battery—the family look to Gorilla Dad to fix it.

He decides when the group moves on, he arbitrates in family disputes, he disciplines the youngsters. He gives a mean hug. He's just like your dad or just like you. He might even look like your dad. Or like you.

Three Happy Meals and a Big Mac Meal, please . . .

Orang Dad

Similarly, your dad might look like an orangutan. Orangutans are different than gorillas, but still pretty much like people. Or, at least, they aspire to be people. Just listen to King Louie in *The Jungle Book*.

They aspire to be people. Just listen to King Louie in *The Jungle Book.*

Orang Dad is one of the cleverest dads in the wild—a fact his palm leaf rain hats and rhythmic singing and dancing can attest to—but his fathering skills leave something to be desired.

He's like a divorced dad. He's the kind of guy who likes to roam around, doesn't live at home, a dad who likes his own space. Wherever he lays his banana, etc. His kids just aren't a big part of his life.

Seems a bit lonely as an example for a human dad, though. Those single men in McDonald's with their kids on a Sunday afternoon—are they our orangs?

> **I'm a natural.**

Chimp Dad

Can chimps out-dad gorillas? Well, chimpanzee society is rough around the edges.

In terms of family, chimps live a soap opera sort of life—long-term relationships peppered with brief liaisons and bastard children, rows and fights, dominant males and scheming subordinates.

It's not easy being a Chimp Dad, having to put up with all the bickering and never getting any time away from the brood. If ever there was a dad who understood the ups and downs of "quality family time," this is him.

If it all sounds too familiar, consider too that Chimp Dad, subject like us to an existence fueled by power and desire, loves his kids.

That's why we look to simian dads: they raise their offspring, they teach them about the forest, keep them tidy, tickle them for fun. These guys know what it's all about. Chimp Dads are natural dads.

> **If ever there was a dad who understood the ups and downs of "quality family time" . . .**

PART
EIGHT

T

The
Dad-
to-Be

The Dad-to-Be

If being a dad is incredibly easy, becoming one is incredibly simple. It is, of course, life-changing. It's life-making too. You wonder and wander around for years, not being able to figure out what life might mean or even if it means anything at all, and then suddenly you're making some of it for yourself. The terminology is easy—you're going to be someone's dad. A role not for the faint of heart; a role for a champion.

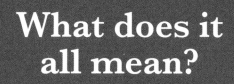

REMEMBER, REMAIN CALM . . .

embrace the panic . . . panic is your friend . . .

Before

Avoiding Panic

You are out in the yard, puffing away on the pipe, sorting out the new shelves for the shed, when your lover comes a-skittering down the path, tear-stained face, used pregnancy indicator strip in one hand, wine in the other.

Panic needs to be ignored. Panic is not what anyone wants from a dad

"Darling," she says, "I'm going to have a baby."

Obviously, your first reactions are likely to be ones of unbounded joy. You might join your wife in having a glass of wine, early though it is. You might delay the shelving and stand talking excitedly in the kitchen about what will need to be done to convert the spare room into a nursery. And after supper and another glass of wine and another go with the ready-rubbed, you feel a warm glow of achievement. Your biology works. You're going to be . . . a dad. Welcome to the gang, kid.

But as you settle back in your armchair, slip off your shoes and put up your feet, you sense a slight discomfort, a lowly voice out of harmony with the glorious chorus of triumph that is the new you. And the lowly voice seems to be getting louder.

This is panic. Panic says things like:

☞ *But what if something goes wrong with the pregnancy?*

☞ *And what if when they do the scan they find something wrong?*

☞ *We can't afford a baby right now. Where's the money going to come from?*

☞ *Am I old or mature enough to be a dad? I'm only forty-five.*

Panic needs to be ignored. Panic is not what anyone wants from a dad. The Dad-to-Be quickly finds sources of panic he didn't know were available. He has to be able to silence them or keep them bearable. He has to live with them.

Oh, you are so cute . . .

Yes, *now* I am cute, but soon you will grow to hate me.

Living with a Beach Ball

Long before any child appears, connubial life begins to change.

For the imminent dad that may involve imminent mom being sick a lot, not being able to tolerate various smells, choosing some interesting meals and so forth.

Pretty soon a little bump appears. And at first it's cute. Along with the grainy ultrasound picture, it is proof of your great achievement. Something is growing, and it's down to you. Half of it is at least. You may find yourself giving the fetus a nickname, say, *Tiny* or *Weeny* or *Little Tadpole of the Rising Moon*, for example. It will soon outgrow this.

★ The last couple of months before Day Zero, when the nursery is painted and the
★ little blankets and sleep suits are safely stowed in the new IKEA drawers, are like
★ living with a woman with a beach ball up her dress.

And the wind of change will certainly blow through the windmills of your mind when you realize that the woman who once looked so irresistible in that black skirt and those heels just shuffled and waddled past in carpet slippers and a sagging tracksuit, sneezing and blowing her nose as though it's some new form of communication.

But, New Man that you are, you can share the experience of beach-ball birthing if you must. The prenatal classes are for couples. Be aware, though, that this is not the meeting where you get up, recite your name and admit to being an alcoholic.

The early classes teach you how to breathe and how to relax. Neither of these skills is usually too taxing for the average dad-in-waiting. One problem is that the classes are often on weeknights. After a full day at work and a rushed meal, it is not unusual once a fifteen-minute relaxation session is over to find three or four prospective dads asleep in their chairs. Heroes, all.

It isn't all sitting around breathing. You get to practice rolling a tennis ball on your partner's back; you get to zap yourself with a TENS machine; you get to watch a video of a woman giving birth in a great big wading pool. You can still hear the screams months after.

Two tips:

If invited to draw a shape with a marker on A4 paper, bear in mind that you may be asked to move your pelvis in this shape later in the session. The man who draws a dodecahedron is headed for injury.

And do not volunteer for anything. Before you know it you'll be linking arms with other exhausted-looking oafs and miming the contractions of a uterus wall as you drive a large blue cushion down into a birth canal dramatically improvised by a computer programmer named Matt and a pet shop manager named Dustin.

It's a grim and sober kind of hokey-cokey that ends when the woman claps her hands and shouts gleefully, "Okay, guys, you were excellent. Weren't they, ladies?" Good preparation only for the humiliations fatherhood brings.

Inhale, exhale, inhale, exhale, inhale, exhale, inhale, exhale, inhale, exhale, inhale, exhale, come on, man, *breathe!*

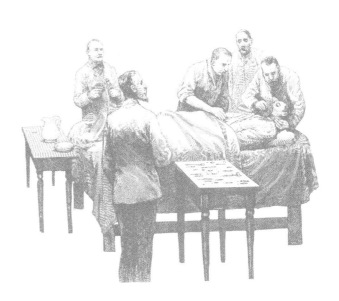

Saying Good-bye to Yourself

Prospective dads, especially those happy to be so, often fail to realize one of the most dramatic aspects of initial fatherhood. Whoever you are or think you are, you no longer will be. Put simply—those days are gone.

Even if someone tells you this, you still don't believe it. Okay, having a child will be a bit more restricting, there'll be some sleepless nights and difficult days, but it can't change you as a person, can it? You are who you are and all that.

Wrong, so very wrong.

What prospective dads ignore is that you are bound to be different; there will be more of you. Yes, more of you. Because the new arrival will be part of you.

If you are what you think and do, and you might be, then it's good-bye to the old you

The prospective mom has known it for a while, but dad will only get it once the bawling bambino is in his hands. If you are what you think and do, and you might be, then it's good-bye to the old you.

You will find yourself thinking things like, "Support the baby's head!" and "The nappy needs changing again?" a lot more than "I think I'll have another beer" or "Another hour in bed sounds beautiful." But all that is mere surface nonsense. The fundamental change is philosophical, existential, even spiritual.

Because you become, paradoxically enough, more and less mortal. You are less mortal because there is a part of you that is something new, outliving you. You feel more mortal because someone has to look after this impossibly fragile life and that someone is you. Your life, as they say, is no longer your own.

★

★

★

It's all a bit spiritual, Daddio.

Money and Worry

You may be born into a family of billionaires, inheriting vast wealth and the structures to keep generating such riches, living a life of opulence and excess and never having to work a day in your life. In which case, any time is fine for having a baby.

For everyone else, there is, as the limerick says, never a right time. The average cost of raising a child is about the price of buying a house. So don't expect your bank account not to notice when a child is born.

Obviously a sensible dad will cut his cloth to suit his cloth availability. Having a Fifth Avenue tailor knocking up the little ones' romper suits is an option, but not a sensible one for most.

At this point many Dads-to-Be will undergo a phenomenon known as squirreling. Squirreling is putting stuff by for leaner times and in this case should include money, alcohol, cigarettes and chocolate, power tools, auto accessories, anything like that. As with life during wartime, all will become increasingly valuable in the postbirth world.

In another way, these aren't financial sacrifices, they are investments. You are investing in the future of your child. After all, someone invested in you.

See you in Barbados!

I can't remember the way!

Oh, darling, why are you such a t***?

During

Avoiding Panic

There are a number of easy ways to eliminate the need for minor panics once labor begins. You should already have the hospital bag packed. Make sure there's gas in the car. Your wife will take several years to see the funny side if she has to deliver at a Mobil twenty-four-hour station because you had to stop for fuel.

A long labor means being stuck at home for hours waiting for some sort of progress

The main source of potential panic early in labor is that the baby will arrive before you get to the delivery room—in the hallway, in the back of the car, at the Mobil station. It all runs through the about-to-be-dad's mind.

And, unless the labor is pretty quick, you can't just whiz down to the hospital. They'll send you back. It's like trying to get in a trendy nightclub—if your contractions aren't good enough, you're not getting in.

A long labor means being stuck at home for hours waiting for some sort of progress. This waiting can give you time to worry. It's best to do something purposeful, like eating a meal, calling close relatives to keep them in touch, checking that the car has gas.

Julian—One of those rare breeds of men who have wide hips, double-jointed elbows and cannot catch. A lecturer in film studies at UCLA and married to a natural birth counselor who is proud to have breastfed their only child up to and slightly beyond its third birthday. Julian couldn't be happier.

Being Useful

Once the process has really gotten going and you're there in the delivery room, it can be intense for dads. It's pretty intense for moms too, don't forget.

Your principal role may be going to get a glass of water, or asking for one of those plastic tubs you puke into

All that husband stuff you happily signed up for at the wedding is really starting to come back to haunt you. Seeing your loved one in pain and being able to do nothing to help but read a newspaper is difficult.

You will want to be useful and supportive; you're certainly getting the easier of the two available rides here and you should bear all that in mind. No need to rush in and start rubbing a tennis ball against anyone's back. Your wife will tell you what she wants you to do.

The nurses often leave you to your own devices, assuming you'll scream or something if you need them, so your principal role may be going to get a glass of water, or asking for one of those plastic tubs you puke into, or going back to the car to have another look for the nature sounds CD.

The Myth of Being Useful

Childbirth is something women do.

There comes a point where the tennis ball, the gas and air, the dextrose tablets all become irrelevant and there's nothing else to fetch (except the camera), and the role of imminent dad is largely not to annoy imminent mom.

This can vary. Some birth-givers will not even notice the father-to-be at the periphery of the natal experience; others may want someone to count and breathe along with them.

You might feel a little stupid sitting there saying, "And breathe and push. And breathe and push. Come on and push, now. Come on. You can push better than that! Push! Hold it! Breathe and breathe and push! And push! You've got to push more! Come on! Keep pushing!" but it's not much of a sacrifice compared to intense bodily trauma.

Think what would have been different without you there. Not much, probably. For centuries, and in many cultures still, dads did not attend the birth. Don't get it into your head that you're needed.

Come on, love, work with me! Yeah, baby!

Service

One aspect of the miracle of birth that really does bring a smile to tight and worried lips is the hospital staff. They do their utmost to introduce a kind of crazy sitcom magic to the whole thing.

They do their utmost to introduce a kind of crazy sitcom magic to the whole thing

They have lots of madcap gags to keep you laughing and stop you from worrying. Look out for the bed that won't tilt then keeps collapsing, the doctor who keeps calling you by someone else's name, the nurse who comes in, turns on a radio tuned to an in-your-face heavy metal station and then leaves. It's so good they must rehearse this stuff.

Watch out for the baby's vital signs machine; this goes on and off to see if you're paying attention. Watch out too for the nurse smiling broadly and asking if you've been shown the tea and coffee facilities while she presses a big red button marked *Emergency*.

In the end, though, they do help you to get your baby safely into the world, and that's the only performance you have to judge. Three cheers!

Blood

Let's not forget that there's a nitty-gritty angle to birth. The angle that fathers-to-be's forefathers didn't have to witness.

Modern Dad's insistence on being there, for whatever reasons, means that he will probably get to see some blood. A surprising amount of blood.

It suddenly seems to be everywhere—on the sheets, the floor, the doctor—and can make you feel a bit squeamish. Fortunately, unless the whole process really has gotten out of hand, it's not your blood. Unfortunately it is the blood of your loved one.

You are now at the furthest point from catalog photographs of impossibly cute infants in gorgeous powder-blue sleep suits and matching nightcaps that it's possible to get. The blood is the *Alien* moment, the wild animal moment. It's dads' language.

Meeting the Beach Ball

You catch a glimpse of a small creature in someone's plastic-gloved hands, pink-skinned but bloody and slimy yellow. The hands wipe some of the slime and blood away with a towel, wrap the little creature tightly into a blanket and hand it to you.

And somehow it's a shock. How can it be? You've been waiting for months, watching the bump grow, looking at the ultrasound pics. But the reality of it is shocking.

There it is—wriggling and twitching, making its thin rasping cry. There it *really* is. And the first time you hold your child, you are meeting it. Whatever you vaguely imagined about what your infant was going to look like disappears in an instant's reality. It's a "How do you do?" moment. The baby in your hands is a puffy, blood-smeared, gurgling person.

Not a beach ball after all.

Oh my God, you're not a beach ball . . .

This is going to be tough . . .

It's a baby!

The New You

Denial, Anger, Acceptance?

So now the roller coaster is up on a stratospheric level. You are calling the relatives, announcing the great news. Close family are coming to the hospital and everywhere you see beaming faces.

Well, now it begins. The next part of your life

You feel like you have dug up a huge diamond and everyone wants to look at it and gasp and laugh. You have both survived, you tell yourself, and everything is okay. No, everything is beautiful.

You. Are. A. DAD.

But watch out. Everyday life, and the sudden disappearance of those feel-good hormones mom has been thriving on for months, could be about to come crashing in.

Suddenly the whole theatrical event of childbirth—the labor, the hospital dash, the adoration of the newborn, the journey home—is done. You get into the house, make a cup of coffee, put the baby in the new bassinet and . . . sit and look at it. What now?

Well, now it begins. The next part of your life. Over the next few weeks you will realize something of the nature of the relentlessness that is dad-hood. The birth exhausted the whole family and there hasn't even been time to recover from that when a new regime, being woken and summoned by a novel thin cry every few hours, takes effect.

And the effect it takes is complete exhaustion. You find yourself wondering if anyone else in the street is awake at 4 a.m. trying to stay upright while wiping milky puke from his neck in the silent darkness.

The traditional route for a traumatic change in life circumstances might be denial-anger-acceptance. In the case of the New Dad this won't do. Acceptance, oddly, comes before denial. And anger, though it might flare, doesn't really feel appropriate—*it's only a baby, for goodness' sake.*

Bodily Functions

A baby cannot keep itself clean. He or she will rely on you to do this. For years.

There is no way past it, you have to deal with urine and excrement, with piss and shit, or, to use your newly acquired vocabulary, wee and poo.

There is no way past it, you have to deal with urine and excrement

In the past, looking after the hygiene of a newborn was solely the responsibility of the mother. Dad could putter about in the garage, wash the car or run down to the bar for a beer and no one thought any the worse of him.

This is no longer the case. The days of the dad, briefly left in charge of a baby, phoning 911 because a diaper needed changing are thankfully gone.

Modern Dad is expected, and expects, to do his bit when it comes to wiping up unpleasant substances and keeping baby stink and stain free. It's all very well in theory. In practice it is and remains grim, day after day. And it certainly doesn't get any better when the child moves from milk to solids.

Something that does bring out that protective, big bear, dad reaction is the simple fragility of babies' little bodies. When you hold them you don't feel powerful, you feel responsible. And when the little body is sick or has a fever or a rash, dad wants to make it better and make it better now. Preferably with mom telling him what to do.

A coughing fit or spate of vomiting—from the baby, that is—can send the New Dad into paroxysms of anxiety and despair. We live physical lives in a physical world and babies do get sick. New Dads get used to doing their best and managing their worry. Driving to the ER at 3 a.m. may be the right thing to do on more than one occasion.

And babies' bodies are busy little things, even when they can't do anything. Having a newborn sleep in the same room as you is a truly wild experience. It's like bedding down with a brood of badgers.

The baby sniffles and snuffles, coughs and hics, wheezes and sighs and moans and burps and farts. Often all at the same time.

Count yourself lucky this book isn't scratch and sniff. I stink.

Choosing a Stroller

Lots of New Dads find themselves feeling oddly and unexpectedly interested in the idea of choosing a stroller.

You don't want to look stupid while you're weaving your way through the bustling aisles of a supermarket

This is because strollers can be thought of as "kit," as vehicles with comparable specs, the whole top trumps thing. They also have a class and status angle. If you're posh, you'll probably want a Silver Cross or a Bugaboo Frog, if you're not, then a simple one will do.

So a New Dad has to identify his position in a number of fields. He has to decide on principles and values for himself—with regard to strollers. Do you go "urban" or "sports"? Are you thinking of a three-wheeler, a buggy, full detachable travel system? Do you know your trunk space? Neutral color? Is it for a girl? Strawberry is nice.

Yes, strollers should be seen as an opportunity to get your mind around some stats—good for talk over a beer with the other dads. And of course you will be seen pushing this contraption around town. You don't want to look stupid while you're weaving your way through the bustling aisles of a supermarket.

Life Without Style

You used to have a lifestyle. You used to do things. You used to go out shopping for stuff; you used to go out to cafés and bars and nightclubs; you used to go away for hectic and hedonistic weekends in picturesque cities.

What happened? You've started falling asleep during the *Ten O'Clock News*; you seem to have time to shop only in CVS and Babies "R" Us; you find the idea of spending a hectic and hedonistic weekend in a picturesque city too much bloody work.

The main reason for the changes in the way you live is that you have become a zombie. And you have become a zombie because you are very, very tired. You are fatigued to a point where you feel, solid macho guy that you are, close to tears for much of the time.

Why won't she stop wailing?

Why won't she stop wailing? Why won't he eat his lunch? They don't sound like big things, but, when you are so tired that your eyes prickle and the spoon of mush that you are trying to get into the food-smeared mouth gets you thinking about a camel passing through the eye of a needle, then you no longer feel in control.

And therein lies the sad, undeniable truth: you no longer are in control. You are the servant of your creation. Achieving pregnancy may have made you feel godlike. Pregnancy over, those tables soon turn. It's Frankenstein time.

Old Ladies in the Street

The great thing about wheeling an infant around in his or her stroller is that lots of people are interested in babies. But be warned, most of these people are women and by far the greater proportion of them will be old.

You can even attract them if you wait in the right places at the right times. Thursday morning is good—it's pension day and the old dears like to get out early and get things done, sensible sorts that they are.

Old ladies in the street have seen life, they know about generations. They are the senior ambassadors of a club to which you have belonged for a mere month or so.

They are a direct bunch too. Not for them the quick glance and understanding smile. No, they stride right up to you, often ignoring you personally, while staring at your offspring and barking questions and observations:

"How old is he?"

Or,

"Oh, she's got lovely hair."

Or,

"Her hands look a bit like claws, don't they?"

All you need to do is smile and look at your firstborn, perhaps answer a few basic questions. Enjoy the adoration the fruit of your loins so richly deserves.

Is he supposed to look like that? Poor child.

Other Ladies

Sometimes you can get to talk to women who are not old. Women you might very much want to talk to if you were not married with a kid.

How

you

doin'?

It sounds better than being snapped at by ancient dearies in house dresses and overcoats, but it isn't. You come away from a few words with some attractive young woman feeling the rub of the new role against your shoulders, disappointed by, and with, yourself. No one said dadness was an easy job.

Da-Da

You have finally achieved the proper state of dad when you let go of the old you, when you have accepted the different way you feel about life, when your paternal values have revealed themselves to you and because of this you are a different, fuller person. And fuller you may continue to get.

Mrs. Dad will one day again become interested in what made you a dad in the first place

★

★ Try to keep some of the old you. While your back and arm muscles may even improve with all the extra bending and lifting your new life requires, dad, tired and frazzled as he is, lives with the constant possibility of becoming a blimp.

New Dads may be tempted to let it all go. Don't. Your kids will need you to be fit and healthy come Field Day, and Mrs. Dad will one day again become interested in what made you a dad in the first place.

PART
NINE

H

How to

Be a Dad

How to Be a Dad

Dads have means and methods. There are dad ways to do things that should come naturally to the family patriarch. They should fit like comfy slippers, or that old Christmas sweater that's okay for gardening. There can sometimes be a bit of chafing, but a strong, upright dad doesn't admit defeat. Anyway, it's not like it's a job you can resign from. You keep trying till either you get it right, mom tells you to stop or you die. If the first of these possibilities sounds the most desirable, heeding advice can help.

How to Wash the Car

There are three basic dad approaches to getting the jalopy shined up again. The easiest car-washing regime is never to wash it. It's a nice, simple idea, but forget it. Even if your car is a black 4x4 that looks as though it's supposed to be dirty, mom will never buy it.

Even if your car is a black 4x4 that looks as though it's supposed to be dirty, Mom will never buy it

The opposite end of the automobile-cleansing timetable schedule is to wash the car diligently every Saturday morning. This is the approach favored by conscientious and organized dads. It scts a good example and is a practice that the kids can join in with so they can feel that they are helping dad, being grown-up, etc.

Washing the car every Saturday goes along with keeping an accurate and complete service history and all receipts for spending on the car during its lifetime.

There is, though, a compromise, in-between, neither-one-thing-nor-the-other approach. This is to put the darned thing through the carwash every couple of months, and just before in-law visits, anything where the impression of a conscientious and organized dad is required. Like all dad-associated tasks, it's about finding your own rhythm.

Papa's got a brand new Flymo!

How to Mow the Lawn

If you think mowing the lawn is a straightforward dad task, prepare to be disabused of your simplistic notion. There are certain basics—you need a lawn, a lawn mower and a non-rain-soaked day. But there is no escaping the fact that mowing the lawn is an important task in a number of ways.

It is a way for dad to survey the outside of his property, be it a mansion with eight acres, a paddock and a beech wood or a two-bedroom terrace with a scabby 12-foot x 15-foot patch of grass in back.

As all dads know, a lawn mower is a frank and forthright means of expressing patriarchal status. Dad A might opt for one of those leather-bucket-seat, high-performance, fuel-injected dragsters; Dad B might only feel the need or the economic ability for a self-assemble, papier-mâché, disposable lawn-chewing system. Shears or

a scythe are not tools of the Twenty-First-Century Dad.

The mowing methods available to dad are stripes or roundels. The first requires cutting parallel lines, the second, concentric circles. Stripes are easier. And it tends to be more fancy dads who go for the roundels.

It is, if your yard is big enough, possible to draw pictures or even write words across your lawn with the mower. The lawn can be a tempting canvas for the expressive dad. Remember, if you fear the wrath of mom, you can always mow over any such artistry when you are finished.

Do be careful, though—faint traces may remain afterward. You don't want *In-Laws Go Home* faintly visible in three-foot letters in front of the house throughout the summer.

Right, got my tools, now how do I get out of the bloody parking lot...

How to DIY

DIY. Yes, hip, hip, hooray for DIY. Or DDD—Definitive, Dad, Domain.

DIY is the heart of Dad Land

DIY is the heart of Dad Land. That landscape of ladders and lino, pale dust sheets and paint cans, in which a tooled-up dad battles the forces of drabness, decay and dilapidation.

The wonderful thing about DIY is that it has so many levels on which a dad can perform his own homeowner heroics. But enough with the alliteration already. Where does all this come from?

Dad's DIY thing owes something to both humanity's hunter-gatherer, cave-dwelling past, as well as the recent predominance of DIY superstores and home-makeover TV shows.

Dad has an instinctive urge to retile the bathroom, fix the guttering and gut the kitchen. It is, in the real world, the case that mom may need to remind dad of these instincts. Spurred to action, few dads can resist the satisfaction of a home improvement task successfully completed.

Not only is DIY comparable with the feminine decorative urge, it overlaps. From the original nursery design in the early years, to the new kitchen and bathroom in married maturity, mom is dad's compass, his architect, designer, furnishings selector, guru. Dad's DIY is often mom's dream.

But all this is to detract from what is essential dad territory. Mom may weigh in with advisory asides, but most of the time DIY is quality dad time. Alone.

Focused on practicalities—the size of the socket anchor, the bubble in the level—dad stands to experience a real sense of purpose. He is improving his home, smoothing rough edges, giving what he can to his family. He is being pure dad.

In this sense, the great thing about DIY is that it's inclusive. The dad who retiles the roof of his bungalow and changes the washer on the dripping bath tap is up there, making the world a better place.

He can wipe his forehead with his sleeve, sigh emphatically, put the tools away and, sweating confidently, smile reassuringly at mom and say something like *Let's have a glass of iced tea, shall we?* safe in the knowledge that she will show her appreciation in her own special way later.

Changing a fuse is nowhere nearly as erotic as repaving the driveway

Obviously this kind of dad reward is not going to be the same regardless of the task performed. Changing a fuse is nowhere nearly as erotic as repaving the driveway or installing a decoratively tiled bathroom.

Damn! It hurts to look this good!

How to Wear a Suit and Tie

Dads are just little boys who have grown up and had families.

Dad, if he gets a moment, can still remember the telling off he got when, age eleven, he came home caked in mud from BMXing through the woods with his friends after a week of intense rain.

He knows all there is to know about wrapping a narrow piece of cloth around his neck and fixing it in a sliding knot

It never occurred to him that clothes didn't magically clean, condition and iron themselves before tucking themselves neatly away in his drawers. Similarly, he couldn't understand his mother's apoplexy when he came home, age thirteen, having ripped holes in both knees of his pants and both elbows of his sweater while out skateboarding with his pals. Why did you have to be smart?

But riding along beside this ragamuffin's adventures was an awareness of life's formality: the school uniform (no grass stains on the knees!), the crazy suit bought for him when he was a pageboy at his uncle's wedding (his first experience of velvet), the jacket only ever worn for visiting grandparents.

Some dads like and feel comfortable with the smart look, many do not.

> # Let's go New Raving.

Many dads shame their kids with their eccentric informality—the golf sweater over the green overalls, the oversized jeans from a charity shop. There are also many who know that the school ethic—ironed shirt, top button fastened, tie tight—carries on into grown-up life.

Over the years dad has tied numerous ties thousands of times. He knows all there is to know about wrapping a narrow piece of cloth around his neck and fixing it in a sliding knot. He knows that there are three options:

- Regular

- Thin

- Fat.

He also knows that ties are subject to something called fashion. Serious dads stick with the regular, whatever fashion might try and dictate. Job interviews, important meetings, a fat or a thin will send the wrong message.

Dad's best tie look is when he's reclined on the sofa, beer in hand, top button undone and a purple silk regular knot loose on his chest. This is what fashion might call "Raw Dad."

How to Chastise/Praise Your Children

Dad knows that children are little animals. They need domesticating. They need humanizing. The trouble is that, wild things though they may be, they are complicated. Children are little proto-people whose brains are undeveloped.

One of dad's trickier jobs is to instill a moral sense into the little creatures

Compared to many animals, newborns are pretty useless. A newborn wildebeest will be able to stand, run and perhaps even escape a predator within hours of its birth; a baby takes several months just to work out how to sit up.

But that isn't really the problem when it comes to baby training. Children need to learn how to behave in a complex social and domestic environment. This is what lies behind every kind of child behavioral issue, whether it is getting a baby not to throw food around the room or getting a teenager to understand why it's not a good idea to say words picked up from a recently acquired rap CD in front of grandma.

As with lots of dad stuff, the Dad Paradox is at work—it gets better and it gets worse. It gets better because eventually your doe-eyed darlings acquire language skills and can be reasoned with. Eventually, however, your beautiful demons use language to fight back.

One of dad's trickier jobs is to instill a moral sense into the little creatures, an ability to weigh your own thoughts and feelings against those of others. Lots of dads fail to do so. It's probably worth it in the end, if only to keep your kids out of jail.

Fortunately for dad, mom has to play a part in this. It is important that parents are united and consistent in terms of praising and chastizing the youngsters, or they will quickly spot the ethical relativity and play one parent against the other. The wild animals that you brought home from the hospital want to learn to be human and they are looking for the boundaries and markers of the social life.

Any dad will tell you that sometimes children are difficult to reason with. They seem unimpressed with the ideas of right and wrong, and any attempts to make them think rationally produce cheeky, provocative responses.

Sometimes they need telling off, they need controlling, they need to just shape up and eat their meal, they need to be quiet, they need to stop hitting their brothers, they need to lay down the crack pipe.

For many generations violence was the accepted means of controlling children. A punch, a slap or a kick from a much bigger and stronger adult usually did the trick. These days, however, this kind of parental influence is frowned upon. Good thing too. Beating up children is what bullies do.

There is, though, some debate about whether a quick smack on the arm or the leg might be an acceptable way of signaling to a child that dad's limit has been well and truly reached and something has to change.

But smacking is not terribly imaginative. Far better to think of some cunning psychological punishment—a link between acceptable behavior and the amount of pocket money your child might expect to receive, for example.

There are usually all sorts of ways that children can be coerced and socialized without a return to the dreadful years of random violence at play school.

How to Chastise/Praise Other People's Children

If training your own rebellious offspring is complicated, other people's children can give just as piercing a headache at times.

★ You have to take into consideration not only what to do but what someone else would

★ think you should do.

★ The best advice is to imagine they are your own—there is firmness and fairness in a dad's heart.

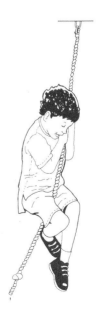

Matthew! I don't care what your parents say! *Not in my house . . .*

Chris

Chris—Lovely sandy-haired Chris is kind
to animals, gives generously to charity, but
unfortunately suffers from dry skin on the elbows.
Tall and lean and not unattractive, Chris has an
annoying habit of reading other people's papers
on the train and apologizing for things that aren't
really his fault. Curiously, Chris was one of the
first men in the Midwest to drink Coke Zero.

Come on kids! Let's P.A.R.T.Y.!

Spike, tell me that's not your old man?

How to Have a Party

Preteens

Everyone likes a party. Children included. Eventually they will get the idea that they could host their own. Clever little things.

There are different kinds of children's parties depending most on how old the child is. From four or five years old to nine or ten, children want one kind of party. From thirteen or fourteen onward, they have a different kind of shindig in mind. As far as dad is concerned, both kinds have nightmarish potential.

Dads, and particularly moms, can get a little competitive when it comes to party time for the young 'uns. Your child's party certainly can't be any less spectacular than the ones he or she has been to, where gifts were lavish and a bouncy castle was only the half of it.

Dad has to venture into the jaw-bitingly expensive world of clowns and magicians, called Bongo or Marvo, and people who tell stories about animals with stupid names and make hats and bicycles out of balloons.

The day itself must, by its very nature—a dozen or more sugared-up five-year-olds running amok, hitting one another, being sick, failing to use the toilet correctly—tends toward the chaotic, and has to be endured.

Dad gets to be thankful that he's not mom, as he watches her making the cake. His job is merely to light the candles and make sure no hyperactive guests suffer burns. And that's a pointer to what your basic aims are—the children, especially yours, have a good time, nothing gets broken and no one gets hurt.

Teens

The basic aims are the same for the teenager party, only the stakes are higher. It is a good idea, if possible, to find a venue that isn't your house. If there is no alternative to having it at home, there are rules and precautions to think about.

It's not necessarily about trusting your own kids. People crash parties, particularly teenagers. Dad knows this; he did it himself. So, assuming and planning for the worst is advisable.

Dad may decide that he needs to be in his house, guarding the castle as it were, from beginning to end, or he may give in to sustained moaning and agree to take mom out somewhere for the evening. If he stays, he is in for a hard night of repelling the uninvited, preventing the drinking and smoking of everyone he sees, and repeatedly discouraging teenage couples from disappearing into bedrooms.

Going out is easier but takes a little more nerve and a little more preparation. How much work would it be to move all the furniture into one, lockable bedroom and to take up the carpets and store them in the garage? Quite a lot.

It may seem like a drastic measure, but the alternative is a future of constantly noticing the dark circle on the living-room carpet where a young lady was once sick, occasionally feeling sad that the grandfather clock no longer works and frequently remembering that the reveller who poured enough of dad's single malt into the fish tank to kill even the snails remains at large.

Even the best party has to stop some time. Have this agreed with your kids in advance. It can't be too early, or they'll feel hard done by. Err on the side of caution; no coming home in time for your regular bedtime.

Once the cinema, the restaurant, and the drink in a local bar are all done, and it's still not the agreed time, you may find yourself with nowhere to go. The most common dad response is to park at the gas station, eat a candy bar and drink some carbonated syrup while listening to the radio. Mom may well be asleep already by this time.

If you are lucky, when you get home your house will be a mess, but one that can be fixed without too much financial and/or emotional expense.

> There must be over three hundred people here!

> God Bless MySpace!

Who said anything about the kids!

How to Do Field Day

The weather has turned out nice again, the school year is coming to an end, and the children are in a high state of excitement. Field Day has it all—Pure Dad Country. And, double bonus, neither mom nor dad has to do any organizing whatsoever.

There is, of course, one thing—competition. Not only are you watching your own kids, trying their little hearts out and panting their way excitedly to those triumphant or abysmal childhood emotional extremes, but you are watching them compete with other children whose parents are also watching. And then the parents get their go. Yes, there's a morsel of edginess on Field Day.

Competition is a funny thing. Dad knows it exists. He sees it every day. The world can be a tough, competitive place. Protecting his children from and introducing them to the harsh ways of the world is a long balancing act for dad.

And then the parents get their go. Yes, there's a morsel of edginess on Field Day

On Field Day he will need both his stories ready. Dad can whoop it up with the kids if they triumph and praise to his heart's content. Or, dad can commiserate and sympathize: *It's not the winning, it's the taking part.* All that stuff is useful and vaguely true.

All of this is subject to one all-important factor: how sporty is Dad? Sportiness is often inherited—just ask racehorse breeders—and for some Dads Field Day is an opportunity to relive youthful conquest and glory. Occasionally you pity their children, but more often than not they get their laurel wreaths, as if genetically bequeathed.

If dad is not of a sporty disposition, it is likely that his offspring will be similarly inept on any fields of dreams. This is where Dad's performance in the hundred-meter egg-and-spoon race matters.

If Dad's children have done themselves some justice and at least not come in last, then Dad must aim to equal this achievement, if not beat it. Your children will enjoy seeing you as a winner as long as they don't see themselves as losers.

If, however, they are losers, then Dad, tempted though he might be to show them how it's done, must also lose. He must throw the fight, rig the game, snaffle the odds. In the last five yards, roared on by the crowd—all the moms and dads, children and teachers—no one else in sight, the finish tape taut and tempting, dad must stumble, the spoon must wobble and the egg must fall. He must walk away from the sports field with the words of Marlon Brando ringing in his ears—yes, dad coulda been a contender.

Dad does this for his child. So that they can both be losers together. If Field Day included video games it would be a whole different story.

I've been training all year for this... and this time I will rule victorious. Oh, yes, this time the egg-and-spoon race is *mine*!

You are a waste of space, Smith! Just like your father was!

How to Handle Parents' Evening

At Parents' Evening you either discover that the teachers don't know the half of it, or that you don't know the half of it. Discussing your child with a teacher is often revealing, not just about Junior, but about dad too.

Whatever your memories of school, do not assume a position of complete hostility to the teaching profession. Go with an open mind; you may hear nothing but honeyed musings about the wondrous qualities of your little genius. Enjoy—it's praise for you too. You brought them up.

You may hear bad news—awkwardly worded assessments that you think imply your child to be some kind of subhuman idiot monster. Challenging behavior, time-management difficulties, problems showing consideration for others—you will get to hear all the current jargon.

Yes, teachers make mistakes and can be quick to judge and slow to reassess, but the likelihood is that if they tell you your daughter is a hideously vicious gang leader who has been terrorizing the school for months, there might be some truth in it. Take it like the dad you are and don't go knee-jerking and out-lashing.

Enjoy—it's praise for you too. You brought them up

In a year or so teacher and pupil may have forgotten each other, not so for father and child. Parents' Evening is a reminder that dads have an ultimate responsibility. The good ones wouldn't have it any other way.

Surprise!

How to Cope with In-Laws

It is obviously a stupid and unhelpful stereotype to categorize all in-laws as problematic, but that's no reason not to use it as a starting point. After all, there are so many possibilities in the relationship between dad and his children's mother's parents for misunderstanding or disagreement.

Many dads are in dire need of coping strategies and assertiveness training...

If it is not the case, if you are a dad who has a fantastic relationship with your in-laws,

and you get on with them like close friends or as well as, or better even than, you get on with your own folks, then good for you.

Many dads are in dire need of coping strategies and assertiveness training. Many dads feel that the home that is their castle is too often infiltrated by a destabilizing Fifth Column—grandma and granddad. Whether maternal or paternal, these two household invaders see it as their business to spoil dad's kids and to comment frequently on how spoiled children are nowadays.

And it is their business.

With his own parents, dad can either cope, having long ago selected his strategies for managing them, or he can keep them at a distance (it's easier for sons). With his in-laws he is on much shakier ground.

Mom likes having them around and it's important for the kids to see them. But he has no way of controlling whether they, at a basic level, get along. They may have decided before the children came along, before the wedding, before any thought of a wedding even, that he just wasn't the right one for their daughter.

The simplest way of avoiding problems with in-laws is to avoid the in-laws themselves

This is not to say that a determined dad can never win over skeptical in-laws. Sometimes he can; sometimes he can't.

So what to do? The simplest way of avoiding problems with in-laws is to avoid the in-laws themselves. Go out. Every time mom says that her mom and dad are coming over, dad can disappear.

The garage and the shed are good if you want to present an active, useful-type-of-guy front, the bar if you don't care. It's an easy-to-use strategy, but it cannot be employed every time or it will be too obvious what's going on.

Avoiding in-laws inside the house (by moving from one room to another) is not recommended. So, when you have to be

in the presence of your other family, when there is no escape, then the one central guiding tenet is . . . do not lose your temper.

No matter how goaded, provoked or patronized a dad feels, if he loses his rag with the in-laws lasting damage may occur. Dad might not be that bothered if he upsets people who annoy him, but mom will be, and dad will end up feeling guilty if he exposes the kids to any edgy family confrontation.

In the case of extreme emergency only, dad should hand over to mom. They are her parents, she can deal with them.

Look, I don't care if you are my mother-in-law, I will fight you to the death!

Monday · Tuesday · Wednesday · Thursday · Friday · Saturday · Dad day

How to Shop

Dad shops in a number of ways. For himself, with the exception of clothes, like the wandering hunter-gatherer he is, he shops best alone.

Car parts, electronics, gardening equipment and tools, he doesn't need anyone else and is faster and more successful in the solitary hunt.

For his clothes he is best off taking mom with him. As long as Dad doesn't let her get fancy, Mom is a sound adviser. She will make you get new slippers but stop you from buying either the cheapest cardboard loafers, which are an excellent value, or the jewel-encrusted Roller-Pimp sneaker. They cost a fortune, but they do play MP3s.

Shopping for the kids is likewise something that mom should probably be involved with.

Dad's role here, right from the early days in Kids "R" Us, is to agree thoughtfully with mom's choice and get his wallet out at the register.

This getting out the wallet can often, ironically, be the enjoyable part of shopping for Mom with Mom.

Buying a new dress or shoes or a coat or anything where Main Street offers Mom an almost infinite number of choices, can be a difficult experience for many dads.

Sitting on the threadbare chair outside the ladies' fitting rooms in Bloomingdale's for forty minutes at a stretch can be frustrating and boring. A sensible dad will take some reading material, or a pencil and pad on which to write lists or draw conservatory designs to nullify the effects of the boredom.

The best way to deal with helping to choose a coat or shoes or a summer top or whatever is simply to pick the second one and insist that you like it but you can't say why. You just like it. You're not really lying. You'll probably get to like it.

The most problematic shopping for dad to do is shopping for mom on his own. It's probably the case that the classic lingerie mistakes are way down the road by the time children arrive. And any self-respecting dad will know mom's dress size and have a vague idea of her likes and dislikes.

But, once he's alone, dad starts to appreciate how tricky it can be deciding between the white blouse with the pink piping on the collar and the pink blouse with the white piping on the collar.

The best thing a dad can do is take notes when out shopping with mom. If she says something is nice, no need to react, but if she says she really likes something, take a quick surreptitious note (in your notebook for lists and designs) of the item, its price, the name of the shop and a rough idea of where in the store it can be found.

That way, come birthday or Christmas, dad is not stuck for ideas, looks like he's been attentive and can always claim, *You said you liked it,* if it's not right.

I'm a dedicated follower of fashion!

A Note on Flowers

Most moms like to receive flowers. They are pretty, they smell nice, they brighten up the nest. Be aware that there is usually at least one kind of flower that mom doesn't like. Make sure you know which it is.

Most moms like to receive flowers. They are pretty, they smell nice, they brighten up the nest

Color selection throws up a number of potential hazards. If going for roses, caution in straying away from the classic red—there

is no worse facial expression than thinly disguised disappointment. Similarly with violets—remember, they are called violets for a reason. A reason moms understand and you do not. Don't be a hero.

The other point to keep in mind is that flowers need to be bought more than once or twice a year (regard birthdays and Mother's Day as mandatory and only let Valentine's slip past if bigger things are in tow. Even then, err on the side of caution) if they are not to look like some sort of apology. Flowers should always be a surprise, but not the kind of surprise that makes someone wary.

You little swine! Come back here with my doughnuts!

How to Handle Teenagers

Teenagers are even harder to handle than toddlers. And they stay up later, so you have to deal with them for longer stretches. Young children understand that they are not yet adults; teenagers have no such ability.

You might think dad would do well to remember his own teenage times. But perhaps not. If he really does some serious remembering, he might end up never trusting or feeling that he knows his children at all.

Teenagers are approaching adulthood and its attendant balancing of freedom and responsibility. They start to want to experience the ways of the grown-ups—sex, cars, alcohol—things many adults struggle to control throughout their lives, so teenagers have no chance.

Like adults they want and need independence, but like children they are still in the business of testing boundaries. Sometimes they don't just test the boundaries, they drive stolen high-performance sports cars right through them while screeching like the demented offsprings of a hyena and a banshee. What to do with them?

Pregnancy

Pregnancy is usually something wonderful and precious. But not always. The words *teenage* and *pregnancy* belong in tut-tutting news stories in tabloids and gossip magazines.

As a dad you can't help knowing that the world-altering sacrifices and responsibilities that a baby brings sit somewhat uneasily with the kind of lifestyle teenagers enjoy. You need to make sure you instill an absolute dread of causing pregnancy or being pregnant into your sons and daughters.

If it doesn't work, or you forget, then get ready to deal with some serious life stuff. Whatever dire reproductional states your offspring may drive themselves to, dad will need to stay calm. A way will be found. Babies make sure of that. Calmness and pragmatism are the keys. Dad does not want to drive his youngsters away.

Arrest

Being telephoned by the police to be informed that Son X or Daughter Y has been arrested is something that a surprising number of dads experience. And a not unequally surprising number of dads, once they arrive at the police station, think, *Oh, yeah, I remember this place.*

For those dads who may be strangers to the penal system, there are a few things to bear in mind. If it's a first offense—shoplifting, drunk and disorderly, trading in endangered species—the long arm of the law will probably want to push your child back to you with a caution and a kind of *Get this amateur out of here* frown.

Go along with their *You won't be so lucky next time* homilies. Do not smile when reunited with your young adult; do not speak on the car ride home; save the disappointment speech for at least a day or two while the child stews; adopt an attitude of barely concealed rage and contempt. It should work on redeemable kids.

If it's a ninth offense and your child greets you in the interview room with an offensive hand gesture, then there's something rotten in the state of dad. Either it's your fault or it's not your fault; the solution is the same.

If the child is at an age where he or she is legally entitled to leave home, this might be good. For a year or two. You can get back together over a pizza when things have calmed down.

If the child is not of an age to fly the coop, there is only one solution—go on one of those TV shows where a bunch of experts deconstruct your family's lives and rebuild you as more efficiently functioning human beings. Plus you get to be notorious for a while.

★

★

★

The police, you say? No, I'm sorry, Officer, he is not *my* son.... He is adopted.

PART
TEN

Where are all
the answers?

Ask Dad

Ask Dad

For the purposes of "sciencelike" inquiry, a specially selected Random Dad (with impeccable credentials) was placed in a large, boring room with thirty children of varying ages who were invited to ask him any questions they wanted. The results are a mixture of the illuminating and the enlightening.

Jennifer, age six, asked:
What is a rainbow?

Dad said: *You've asked a very interesting question. And fortuitously I know the answer. A rainbow only happens when it is sunny and raining at the same time, doesn't it? So, sunshine plus rain equals rainbow.*

The reason that a rainbow is lots of different colors is that sunshine is made up of lots of different colors. But you can only see them when it's raining. Why is it curved? It's curved because…light's…bendy?

Gail, age five, asked:
Where does the sun go?

Dad said: *It doesn't really go anywhere. In our experience, in terms of what we see, in a poetic sense, if you like, it does go. The end of the day, darkness, the sleep of humanity, its nightmares and dreams, the fluctuation between the great polarity that dominates our existence. Yes, in some senses, the sun goes.*

Actually, the world is turning and for a few hours we are just on the wrong side of the world to see it. I'd like to give you a follow-up question, Gail, but I've made myself feel a bit dizzy. Just a second.

Samantha, age three, asked:
Where do babies come from?

Dad said: *I don't know. I've been wondering that. Have you asked your mother? She said a baby grows from a seed? That doesn't sound very likely to me. You were a baby quite recently—can you remember where you came from? Yes, it is hard to remember. Oh, yes, they are lovely shoes.*

Darren, age eight, asked:
What is it like being drunk?

Dad said: *You're eight and you're asking me? Well, if you really don't know already, there are different sorts of being drunk. You drink a few beers and you can be loose, tipsy or merry, and that's good fun.*

You drink a few more beers and you can be toasted or sloshed, and that is good fun too.

You keep drinking those beers and you can be bombed, wrecked, smashed, hammered or wasted, and then it's not quite such good fun.

And if you manage to keep drinking, you can be out of order, well out of order or unconscious, and that's no fun at all. But I still think you know all this already. Am I right? Am I?

Jane, age eleven, asked:
Who invented money?

Dad said: *What a brilliant question. You're probably some sort of wunderkind, aren't you? Who invented money? Beats me. Wish I had. I'd be pretty rich by now, huh? Wow.*

I've never been asked that before. Are your parents teachers or something? My children never asked me that. Definitely a top notch question. If you're ever up for adoption, here's my card.

Wayne, age thirteen, asked:
Why can't children drive cars?

Dad said: *Children do drive cars. Every time I'm on the roads there seem to be children driving cars wherever I look. They just happen to be children between seventeen and thirty.*

You just have to wait your turn. Why not try go-karting? Children can do that. Go-karts are just cars without shells. And being a car owner is just too expensive for most kids. Don't even think about driving a car until you've got a job. Possibly two.

Adam, age twelve, asked:
Why don't boys wear dresses?

Dad said: *The thing about your question is that I feel I should know why you are asking before I answer it. You might just be asking out of a mild curiosity, having observed one of life's anomalies; or you might be looking for me to persuade or dissuade you from something you've been thinking about for a while.*

I know answering a question with a question is not generally the done thing, but in response to your inquiry—does it matter?

Jake, age seven, asked:
Why are people different colors?

Dad said: *The simple answer, Jake, is that people's color depends on where they come from, or where their families came from. Pink people come from Europe, brown people come from India, very brown people come from Africa. Or their mommies and daddies did.*

There is a more complicated answer to do with geography and sunlight and vitamin A and melanin. But I don't really understand it. The thing to know is that you can't tell what people are like from their color— people don't choose the color of their skin, eyes or hair. Occasionally you have to factor in jaundice.

Stephanie, age eight, asked:
Why do I hate people?

Dad said: *You don't hate people. No, you don't…Calm down….No, you don't hate everyone…Come on…Okay, here's a tissue…There…See? It's not so terrible, is it?*

Look. Life can be difficult sometimes. We have to try to balance what we want with what other people want. And that's not always easy. If things don't go the way you want, then it's only natural to feel bad. But you won't feel bad forever.

Try to think nice thoughts. Think about the things you like.…Yes, I'm sure there's a candy store near here. Yes, horses are nice. They are a good thing to think about.

Ian—The runt of the litter, and no taller than 5 feet 8 inches, Ian has never knowingly filled a shirt. Maryland based, but with a southern twinge to his accent, he likes to travel to work in an American-built car and would never consider playing squash. Or any other racket sports. Although prone to constipation, when buying his own toilet paper will almost always choose two ply.

Terry, age six, asked:
Why don't women have mustaches?

Dad said: *Terry, my man, you have a lot to learn. Some women do have mustaches. They tend not to have beards, though. How your hair grows is down to hormones, which are like chemicals in your body, and men have chemicals that make them grow beards and women don't.*

It's really so you can be sure who is a man and who is a woman. If you're going to ask why men shave—I don't know. For my money, a lustrous beard is a beautiful addition to any face.

Sean, age eight, asked:
Where do babies come from?

Dad said: *This one again. Well, a kid your age, you probably have some idea already. Have the older boys told you something on the playground? They have? And you want me to tell you if it's true.*

I bet what they told you sounds possible but incredibly horrible. It's true. Forget about it for a couple of years, though. Between now and you growing a beard, there is lots of time to get used to crazy things.

Laura, age four, asked:
Why does Uncle Peter smell like burning?

Dad said: *I don't know Uncle Peter. For all I know he may be some kind of pyromaniac. But I suspect he is probably a smoker. Smoking is something you can do when you grow up. It makes you look big and cool, but it kills you.*

My advice is to get your parents to agree to giving you five hundred dollars if you don't smoke a cigarette before your twenty-first birthday. Stay healthy and make money. I know you're only four, but it's smart to plan ahead.

Emma, age seven, asked:
Why aren't there dinosaurs anymore?

Dad said: *There are three answers to your question. The first is that there are still lots of dinosaurs everywhere. All the dinosaurs turned into birds a long time before you were born. So the sky is full of dinosaurs.*

The second answer is that they all died because the world got too cold or too hot for them.

The third answer is that there are some proper big dinosaurs still alive. They live on an island somewhere near Costa Rica.

Carl, age ten, asked:
Why do some families have more children than others?

Dad said: *Good question, young man. The answer is that lots of things affect how many children there are in a family. I mean, it's sociology, isn't it? Demographics, relative wealth, health care, culture, religion.*

It's big stuff. You're asking a big question. And then there's just luck. Take as an example the niece of this guy at work, Gus. His niece…Where's he gone? Where did that boy go?

Heather, age four, asked:
Why do pets die?

Dad said: *And not only pets. No, what I mean to say is that pets have different lives. They live here for a while and then they die and their spirits go to heaven.*

Up in heaven pets get to play around and have fun forever. What do you think, Heather? Think I could get a coffee here? No, I don't think they have school in heaven.

Hailey, age six, asked:
Why do people go to work?

Dad said: *The bitter truth, Hailey, my young friend, is that not everybody goes to work. There are people who can't find a job and they want to work. Then there are people who go to work but don't want to. Then there are people who don't work and don't want to work.*

The key ingredient in all this is money. If you haven't got any money you need to work; if you have lots of money you don't. What does your dad do? A movie star? Really? What's his name? Yes, I saw that one. *He*'s your dad? Wow. Well, all that stuff I just told you? You don't need to know it.

Russell, age nine, asked:
Why do people get old?

Dad said: *You're hitting a nail on its head there, Russell. And you're opening up a philosophical can of worms with that nail. Why do people get old? Processes corrupt, stuff degenerates, everything decays, it doesn't really matter.*

What you're actually asking is whether you will ever be able to accept life's icy background music—the ticking of the clock, the blur of the seasons, the lines yet to appear on your face, your mortality.

Am I right? No. You just want to know why people get old. Well, don't worry, Russell, by the time you're old they'll have cured it and you'll be able to live forever. Yeah, cool.

Alice, age three, asked:
Why do people tell lies?

Dad said: *If you think about it, young lady, you probably already know the answer to that question. Why do you tell lies? Are you sure? Never? Never ever? No, don't cry. There's no need to cry. Lord above. I didn't say you were a liar….No I didn't…I'm not calling you a liar, I'm merely contradicting you…It's not the same thing at all.*

Gavin, age eleven, asked:
Why are there wars?

Dad said: *I don't know. It seems like everyone has to hate someone. If you figure this one out, let me know.*

Megan, age three, asked:
Why can't I have a puppy?

Dad said: *You might be able to have a puppy, but perhaps not just yet. Puppies need looking after and you're not quite old enough to take care of one right now. Maybe in a few years or so. Yes, the same goes for a rabbit. Yes, and a guinea pig. Yes, and a hamster. Yes, and a pony. And the same for a dinosaur.*

Mavis, age nine, asked:
Why can't I have the same sneakers as my friends?

Dad said: *There are a couple of ways of approaching this. There might be a very simple reason for you not being able to have the same sneakers as your friends. Your parents might not have the money to pay for them. Or the reasons could be more complicated.*

They might have the money but need it to buy other things—fish sticks, bananas, dishwashing soap. They might have the money but think that the sneakers are not very nice and that they wouldn't look good on you. They might just want you to know that you don't have to do everything your friends do or have everything they have.

Which ones do you want anyway? Show me a picture. Oh, they're awesome. No, you're right—they're cool. They'd definitely suit you. You should ask your parents to get you those. Do they do them in a size ten, do you think?

Janice, age eleven, asked:
Why are boys so stupid?

Dad said: *I don't want to depress you, but you might find yourself asking that question not infrequently throughout your life. Not infrequently means quite often. Yes, I should have said that. Yes, it's probably because I'm a man.*

The thing is, Janice, that eventually, although a long time after girls, boys stop being stupid and can even end up being reasonable. Don't worry too much about it. In a few years they will stop seeming quite so stupid and start to seem amusing and even...interesting.

I don't expect you to believe me. But that's what happens.

Kirk, age ten, asked:
Will I ever like my sister?

Dad said: *Yes, you will. Probably. There are no guarantees, my friend. The chances are that the reasons you don't like your sister at the moment will disappear. You probably fight over who has what and who gets attention when.*

Once you're all grown up, you'll have your own life and your own things and you won't need so much attention. She did what? No. Oh, no. That makes things very different. Yes. Did they? Well, I suppose that's what social workers are for.

Steven, age six, asked:
Will my dad ever be able to play football?

Dad said: *No, Steven, he won't. But don't worry about that. Because I know for a fact that your dad can do things that nobody else's dad can. I don't know what they are. You'll have to find out.*

James, age fourteen, asked:
Where do babies come from?

Dad said: *Don't pretend to me that you don't know. You should concentrate your thinking on how to stop babies coming from wherever it is they come from. Now go outside and play.*

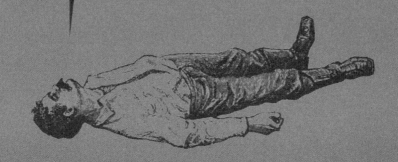

PART
eleven

Dad's Recipes

Dad's Recipes

Historically, the kitchen is hostile turf for dads. It is perfumed with potpourri, full of French words like *flambé*, *fricassé* and *mayonnaise* and is the indisputable fortress of Mrs. Dad. However, there have been a few who have braved this enemy ground, stared danger in the face and managed to rustle up beautiful and tasty snacks. What follows is a compendium of their soon-to-be famous work. Salute these heroes; they live in glory.

Beer Bread

Ingredients:

3 cups self-rising flour (DO NOT USE
ALL-PURPOSE FLOUR)

2 tablespoons sugar

1 can beer

Method:

Grease your loaf pan with nonstick spray
or by rubbing butter on it with a paper
towel. Measure out 3 cups of flour in a large
mixing bowl and sprinkle the sugar on the
top. Pour in about half the beer and mix.
(Do not drink the other half of the beer.)
When it's pretty well mixed, slowly add the
rest of the beer while continuing to mix.

When it has reached the consistency of goo,
scrape the dough into your loaf pan and
bake at 350°F for 55 to 60 minutes. The top
will get golden brown and crispy when it's
done.

Remove your masterpiece from the oven and
let it cool for 5 to 10 minutes, then dump it
out of the pan.

Egg in a Bag

Ingredients:

1 big pot of boiling water
1 large plastic Ziploc bag
4 eggs

(Optional)
cheese
onions
ham
jalapenos
tomatoes
anything else that you might like in an omelet

Method:

Crack the egg into the bag and add the other
desired ingredients. Shake and mix (I mean,
the bag). Then drop the bag in the boiling
water, and turn off the heat. If you have a
lid for the pan, cover the pot, but if you're
roughing it, the lid is optional.

Cook the ingredients through an entire
segment of *SportsCenter* (about 15 to 20
minutes), and you'll have a tasty egg
scramble with all your favorite ingredients,
without the mess.

Variations:

If you're making this to impress Mrs. Dad,
you may also want to use a plate and fork.

Le Pie Royale

Ingredients:

1 large Pot Pie

1 small jar of French Dijon mustard

1 glass chilled 2% milk

Method:

Remove pie from butter compartment in door of fridge. Place on small bread board. Cut pie into 8 equal slices, dabbing mustard carefully on to peak of each slice. Greet each mouthful with a gulp of milk. Ah, sensational.

Founded:

Mark Grady circa 1998—somewhere in those long hours between dinner and breakfast the next day.

Laziness factor: 9/10

Salmon Crumble

Ingredients:

1 can of salmon

1 bag of salted chips

1 can chopped tomatoes

Method:

Open cans and fold salmon chunks into tomatoes. Shape into salmon shape and decant into baking tray. Shake bag of chips over salmon. Place in oven, preheated to gas mark whatever. Leave until brown. Serve to family with pride.

Founded:

Ian Barham, on paternity leave, Cincinnati, 1989. Having recently had his first child, Ian has not slept a full night in over three weeks.

Laziness factor: 3/10

The Tower of Power

Ingredients:

1 minute corner of rye bread

1 jar of smooth peanut butter

Method:

Using full natural bulk of a mature grown dad, block the family's view of this most clandestine of recipes. Carefully remove 1-inch square piece of rye bread from loaf—rye or thick wheat bread gives far better grip—then teaspoon smooth tower of PB onto square. Drop the load straight into open mouth, chew once and swallow.

Founded:

Graham Samuel in 1971 as part of experiment into ingesting most amount of calories in shortest amount of time.

Laziness rating: 9/10

The Dirty Guacamole

Ingredients:

1 tub of supermarket guacamole

Method:

Take index and middle finger and make the shape of a gun. Remove lid from container (with other hand) and insert "gun" into guac. Make a quick, clean sweep around the perimeter until the guac is up to second joint of index finger. Remove, bend "gun" into spoon shape and place in mouth.

Founded:

12:35 a.m. Tijuana, Pepe Ramirez returns from night out salsaing with his mamacita to discover lone, slightly fizzy container of guacamole in fridge. "Andale, mi tummy estas rumblato."

Laziness rating: 10/10

The Banana Splat

Ingredients:

2 large bananas

1 can of whipped cream

1 pudding cup

1 milk chocolate bar, large

sprinkles

1 marachino cherry

Method:

Slice both bananas into inch-wide slices, deposit in bowl. Deposit pudding cup into bowl. Break chocolate bar into equal segments, deposit in bowl. Spray on pyramid of whipped cream, then add sprinkles generously. Lavish with cherry. Shovel into mouth with dessert spoon.

Founded:

Sunday afternoon, in the 4:30 dessert window, by Sammy Barker, attorney and father of three.

Laziness rating: 4/10

Sealed with a Hiss

Ingredients:

2 slices of white toast

2 raw eggs

4 strips of bacon

1 George Foreman grill

Method:

Insert 1 slice of white toast into the George Foreman, crack two eggs. Use large knife to salvage any overspill back onto bread base. Delicately place strips of bacon into egg mixture and depress remaining slice o' white bread onto top. Clip top of George Foreman into place. Cook until edible.

Founded:

Saturday morning hangover moment results in this most surprising of breakfast treats.

Laziness rating: 5/10

Epilogue

So there it is. The whys, the wherefores, the hows and the whens. The big fajita, the cookie cutter, the master-blaster. The daddy.

And what have we learned? That the life of Dad is one heck of a journey, one zooming roller-coaster trip, an upside-down parabola, the trajectory of a stone thrown into the wind, an arrow fired at the sun. Yes, indeed, it would seem that being Dad is some adventure.

Lest we forget, Dad is a spiritual endeavor too—a life-creating, life-affirming, life-questioning pursuit. It makes ordinary men great and great men superhuman. It makes you cry, hoot, swear, giggle, shout, chortle, scream, laugh, shriek…and then love. It is what you make of it, and what it makes of you.

And then, one day, it's over. The flock flies the coop. The shepherd is left bereft.

And yet he isn't. They will be back, most likely more than he thought possible.

There will be false starts, money stuff, broken hearts. Once that door closes something happens and being Dad becomes part nostalgia. With luck another role waits in the future:

Granddad. The King of Dad.